Léonard de Vinci.
La Joconde.

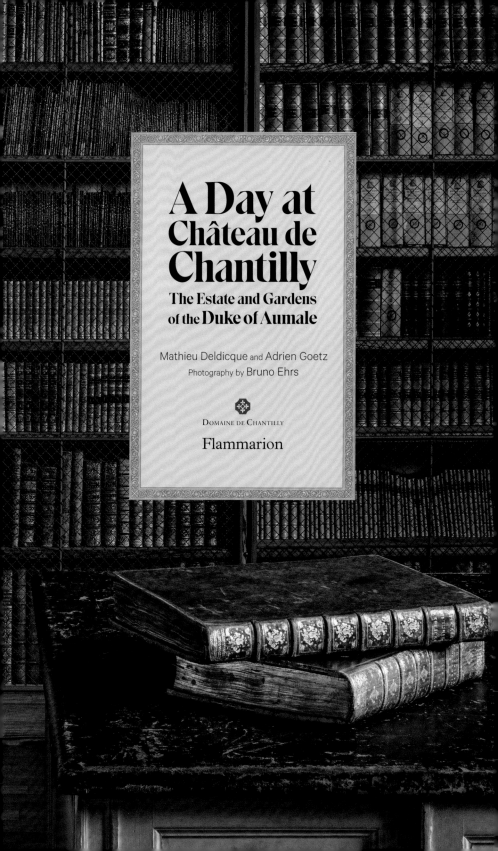

A Day at Château de Chantilly

The Estate and Gardens of the Duke of Aumale

Mathieu Deldicque and Adrien Goetz

Photography by Bruno Ehrs

DOMAINE DE CHANTILLY

Flammarion

Contents

PAGE 1
Detail of woodwork with the
monograph of Henri of Orléans,
Duke of Aumale.

PAGES 2–3
The Library and the *Nude
Mona Lisa*, by Leonardo da Vinci
(or his studio).

PAGES 4–5
The estate's two châteaux: on
the left is the one built by the
Connétable de Montmorency,
on the right the one rebuilt by
the Duke of Aumale.

BACKGROUND IMAGE
Anne de Montmorency,
engraving by Jean Picart.

FACING PAGE
The terrace with the equestrian
statue of the Connétable de
Montmorency, commissioned
from sculptor Paul Dubois
by the Duke of Aumale in 1886.

The *très riches heures* of the Duke of Aumale

Xavier Darcos, Chancellor, Institut de France

During formal sessions of the five academies comprising the Institut de France, as members enter their august premises on the Seine to the sound of the drums of the Garde Républicaine, they pass before a bust of Prince Henri of Orléans, Duke of Aumale. Their minds inevitably turn toward that extraordinary man, who not only was elected to three of the academies (the Académie Française, the Académie des Beaux-Arts, and the Académie des Sciences Morales et Politiques), but also decided to endow future generations with his most precious possessions by entrusting his estate of Chantilly to the institute. Currently three of us—members of the three academies he belonged to—are specifically charged with guarding his treasures.

Chantilly is miraculous. This highly original museum, which is also a palace with extensive grounds and stables, bears no comparison to other French museums. Nor is it like stately homes in Britain, despite a similarly imposing presence and "modern" comforts, in so far as Chantilly embodies, above all, the French spirit. Nor, finally, is it like the lavish mansions built by wealthy Americans in Newport, Rhode Island, during the same years the prince was completing his life's work.

Chantilly is unique. It dazzles even as it encourages the mind to travel. It is both a little taste of Italy (with a collection that rivals those in Naples and Rome) and a monumental palace like Versailles (where King Louis-Philippe established a museum of paintings and sculptures that recounted the saga of the French nation). Yet it is also a little Tower of London harboring family jewels, with richly storied gardens that, beneath a mantle of snow, may even appear Russian or Scandinavian.

The Duke of Aumale would have warmed to Bruno Ehrs, a photographer already familiar with Swedish castles and royal courts. In the pages that follow, Ehrs's photos capture the protean spirit of the premises, revealing every facet of this sparkling diamond in a forest setting. Meanwhile, the two authors of the text take us on a tour that lasts one timeless, poetic day. Mathieu Deldicque—a former pupil of École nationale des chartes in Paris, and curator at Chantilly—and Adrien Goetz—a member of the Institut de France and a specialist in nineteenth-century art—lead us through the rooms of the Condé Museum, which they know so well. They also show us the gardens and stables, and recall the hunts of yore. We sense that they understand and love Prince Henri, the son of a king, who, during years of exile in England, dreamed of this perfect setting and doggedly prepared to recover it. The authors admire the man who loved Raphael and Poussin yet who also bought works by Delacroix, Ingres, and Meissonnier. They pay tribute to the duke who, for the good of his country, sought to reincarnate his hero, the Grand Condé (victorious defender of France at the battle of Rocroi in 1643) yet who never forgot that his own father fought under the republican flag during the French Revolution.

The Duke of Aumale's meticulous will was very exacting, stipulating that nothing can be altered in this, his life's work, the château de Chantilly. Having totally refashioned what he inherited, he became its sole maker. His prohibition has prevented any alteration of its perfection. Yet nothing is "fossilized" here, because the founder's philosophy, once understood, must be perpetuated through activities—restoring works, holding major exhibitions, making relevant acquisitions, organizing events for garden and flower specialists, and hosting dinners for patrons and donors. All these efforts bring Chantilly to life in the twenty-first century, making it sparkle today.

This book opens like an illuminated manuscript, full of treasures such as the *Très Riches Heures*: paintings and drawings worthy of the Louvre, furniture equaling anything at Buckingham Palace or the Wallace Collection, and a hamlet that rivals the Trianon, not to mention a racecourse and grandstand whose heights of elegance can make races feel like Ascot. Everything has been preserved, everything is intact—yet everything is vibrantly alive.

These are the magnificent prince's *très riches heures*. ∎

The Last of the Princes

His Royal Highness Prince Henri of Orléans, Duke of Aumale, truly loved France—during two periods of exile, his country seemed like a distant princess he yearned to rejoin. The duke was a curious, unusual man who played a special role in French history. The son of King Louis-Philippe, he lived through the major upheavals of the nineteenth century—a series of regime changes in France, the sudden arrival of modernity in all realms of life, and the victorious rise of burghers, industrialists, and merchants. Politically liberal, the Duke of Aumale observed and analyzed contemporary developments with an aloofness stemming from his great learning and his special status above all polemics and political parties. During the Third Republic, he resembled the statue of the Connétable de Montmorency that greets visitors to Chantilly: on horseback, with raised sword. In the minds of the people of the day, he was the last of the princes, one who came to terms with the establishment of a republic. Some even thought he could be elected president after the fall of Napoleon III, but he didn't run for office. He seemed to prefigure the Prince of Salina, the protagonist of Lampedusa's novel *The Leopard,* made into an unforgettable film by Visconti. His penchant for the most glorious periods of the past was matched by a passion, typical of his times, for collecting things: not only old masters but also contemporary paintings, objets d'art (in the tradition of cabinets of curiosities), lavish furniture with glamorous histories, illuminated manuscripts, and incunabula and other rare books, all of which gave new meaning to his historic château at Chantilly. Although the old castle was largely destroyed in the closing years of the French Revolution, the Duke of Aumale rebuilt it, and ultimately bequeathed it to the Institut de France, that "parliament of scholars."

Toward the end of his life, on Sundays he enjoyed hosting receptions on his estate—a kind of "complete, variegated monument to French art"—to which he invited everyone of importance in France, ranging from princes in his own large

family, to members of the three academies to which he belonged, to writers, artists, and politicians. He welcomed book-lovers, collectors, descendants of grand ancien-régime families, and nouveaux riches like Anna Gould (daughter of the wealthiest man in the United States) and her husband, Count Boni de Castellane. The duke's mother, Queen Maria Amelia, was a princess of the Two-Sicilies branch of the extended Bourbon family, as well as the niece of Marie-Antoinette. His father, King Louis-Philippe, was the son of the politically radical Duke of Orléans who took the title Philippe-Égalité during the French Revolution and even voted to execute his own cousin, King Louis XVI, guillotined in 1793. At Chantilly, the French royal fleur-de-lis is combined with the republican tricolored flag. The duke's fascination with "old memories"—with the life once led there and its "sweet pleasures," to quote Talleyrand (whose portrait hangs in the château)—was matched by strong hopes for the future. "Hope" (Espérance) was the motto of the Bourbons, which the Duke of Aumale adopted as his own and inscribed more or less everywhere.

As a next-to-last son, the duke played no dynastic role. But he was very rich: his godfather, the last prince of Condé (from the younger branch of the royal family), bequeathed him vast forest domains as well as the ruins of Chantilly, where there miraculously survived the Petit Château (built in the sixteenth century by architect Jean Bullant) and the Grand Apartments with their magnificent eighteenth-century interiors. These damaged buildings perpetuated the memory of the Orgemont family, who had handed the property down to the Montmorency and, later, Condé families.

In July 1830 the Bourbon king Charles X was overthrown and Louis-Philippe of Orléans was named "King of the French." The Orléans family, descended from Louis XIV's brother, thereby ascended to the throne. Young Henri was an intelligent child who first attended classes at school with other students, then completed his education with a youthful tutor, Alfred Cuvillier-Fleury, who became a friend and adviser. The entire Orléans family loved the arts. The duke's older brother was a collector with eclectic tastes, maintaining a balance between Ingres, Delacroix, Delaroche, and the Orientalists, while his sister Marie was a sculptor; other siblings did drawings, watercolors, and eventually photography.

FACING PAGE
The Duke of Aumale and the Prince of Joinville at Claremont, photograph by Antoine François Jean Claudet. The Duke of Aumale (left) poses here with his brother, the Prince of Joinville. This photograph was taken in 1848, at the start of their exile, which lasted until 1871.

"Wouldn't it be great luck today to own the home of the Connétable de Montmorency just as it existed in his day? That's what I want to do with Chantilly."

Henri of Orléans, Duke of Aumale

"I feel that your royalty is no longer political; it has now become historical. My Republic is not troubled by that. You are part of France's grandeur, and I am very fond of you."

Victor Hugo to the Duke of Aumale, July 17, 1880

The future seemed to belong to the dazzling house of Orléans once it had replaced the main royal branch following the exile of Charles X, Louis XVI's last surviving brother.

In 1884, the Duke of Aumale bequeathed Chantilly to the Institut de France. At that point he had witnessed the death of all seven of his children, some at birth, others in their youth; he had also lost his wife in addition to the two sons who were supposed to carry on his line. One son was styled the Prince of Condé (1845–1866); the other, the Duke of Guise (1854–1872). He decided that Chantilly, which he had constantly modified and embellished, should remain in the state it was found on the day of his death. As a young man, Aumale's imagination had been gripped by Pompeii and Herculaneum—his estate would be a work of art fashioned by himself, one that people could enter, centuries after his death, as though he himself had just left. His museum of a home would be an intact fragment of the past, what art historian Bruno Foucart called a "still-attainable Atlantis." Chantilly's originality stems from these historical musings, which even today encourage us to dally and dream. The château and its grounds are composed like an autobiography that can also be read as a family tree. Strolling through it with guests, Prince Henri could see himself in everything, as in a mirror. Other museums across the world are similarly designed to spur remembrance of things past as we wander through them, such as the Wallace Collection in London, the Isabelle Stewart Gardner Museum in Boston, and the Frick Collection in New York.

The Duke of Aumale's first career was a military one. He fought in Algeria, becoming the French hero of the capture of Abdelkader's camp in 1843. (This victory was commemorated in a panoramic painting by Horace Vernet hung in the historic rooms of the renovated château de Versailles, which were turned into a museum of "France's glorious past.") At Chantilly, the duke owned a large portrait of Abdelkader, the famous Algerian leader, in exile in France—all honor to the defeated.

Even as Europe's Catholic monarchies, remaining loyal to the senior Bourbon branch of France's royal family, imposed a "matrimonial blockade" on the Orléans branch, the Duke of Aumale married his first cousin, Maria Carolina Augusta of Bourbon–Two Sicilies in 1844. He had highly refined rooms fitted out for her in the Petit Château, meeting modern tastes and standards of comfort. The couple hardly had time to enjoy them, for the revolution of 1848 forced King Louis-Philippe and his family into exile. In England, at Orléans House near Twickenham, Henri developed a fascination with everything related to his home country. With time on his hands, he began the serious undertaking of writing scholarly articles and books, such as a monumental, seven-volume *History of the Princes of Condé* and a study of Julius Caesar's siege of Alésia (a subject that also fascinated Emperor Napoleon III, as Henri knew). From a distance he monitored his château in Chantilly (which had been sold to straw men loyal to him) and he tirelessly enlarged his collections in the hope of repatriating them some day. He bought shares in various French publications and envisaged himself as an influential figure. In 1871, the year the law exiling him was rescinded, he was elected as a representative of the Chantilly region; he recovered his rank of general the following year, and in 1873 he was chief judge at the trial of Marshal Bazaine, accused of the cowardly surrender of the city of Metz, which hastened France's defeat in the Franco-Prussian war. When Bazaine defended himself by explaining that the French government no longer existed by the time he surrendered, the duke's characteristic response became famous: "*France* still existed."

He went into exile again in 1886, the Republic having struck him off the army staff. The government was wary of members of the former ruling houses. He had begun rebuilding the main château at Chantilly in 1875, on the foundations of the old one. The architect chosen by the duke was more malleable than Viollet-le-Duc (hired by Napoleon III to recast Pierrefonds as a medieval citadel), namely Honoré Daumet, a winner of the Prix de Rome and a member of the Académie des Beaux-Arts since 1855. Daumet devised—with constant advice from the duke, whom we can easily imagine poring over the plans—an original version of a Renaissance dwelling. Unlike other "revival" châteaux then being built in Europe— brick-and-stone manors, variations on the Petit Trianon, etc.—Chantilly was not regular in plan. Asymmetry reigned, and diagonals were favored over right angles, evoking architecture prior to the days of Le Vau and Mansart, and poetry prior to Malherbe. Chantilly was a contrast to all the pastiches of Versailles. Similarly, the "Condé Museum," hidden in the midst of a forest, differed from the fine-arts palaces then populating most major cities. Nothing about it was

FACING PAGE
An accurate depiction of the château before the damage done by the French Revolution. In front is the Petit Château, built in the sixteenth century, which remained almost intact. In contrast, the Grand Château behind was razed to its foundations and rebuilt in a Renaissance-revival style by the Duke of Aumale from the 1870s onward.

PAGES 23–24
The Château de Chantilly Seen from the Aviary Bridge in 1872, prior to Reconstruction of the Grand Château, photograph by Claudius Couton.

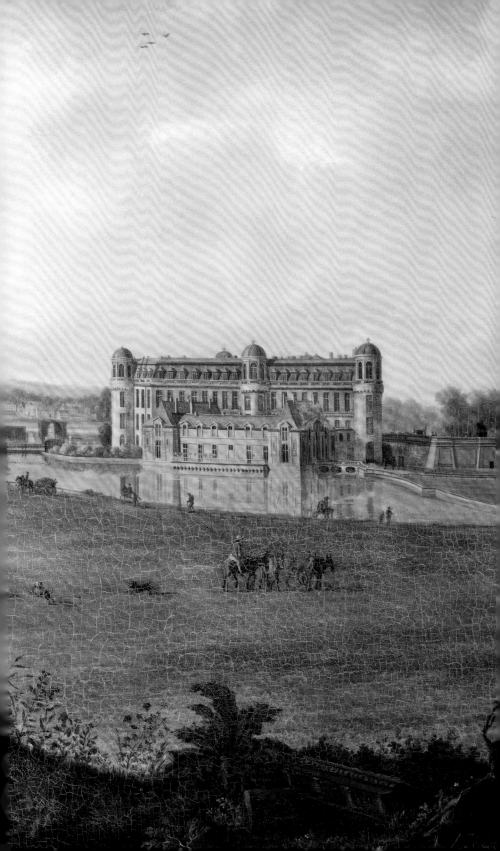

rational—delight overruled pedagogy. The Gallery of Painting, the Tribune, the Santuario, and the rooms crowded with paintings were anything but a course in art history. They reflected the fancy of the last of the princes, who returned to France in 1889 and wanted to bequeath to the nation everything he loved—along with his viewpoint.

He died in 1897 at his estate in Lo Zucco, Sicily. His remains, draped in the republican tricolor, were returned to Paris. A funeral mass was held in the church of La Madeleine prior to his burial in the royal chapel of Dreux (where Louis-Philippe and his descendants lie). It was sculptor Paul Dubois, who did the equestrian statue of the Connétable de Montmorency in front of the château, who executed the marble recumbent figure of the duke in his general's uniform. ■

FACING PAGE
The entrance pavilion to the Renaissance-style Petit Château, silhouetting the chapel steeple and the equestrian statue on the terrace.

RIGHT
Miniature painted by Jean Fouquet (mid-fifteenth century) for the *Hours of Étienne Chevalier*. One of the magi has the features of King Charles VII.

PAGES 28–29
The façade of the Petit Château seen from the Aviary Garden.

PAGE 30
Letter from the Institut de France to the Duke of Aumale, thanking him for his bequest of Chantilly.

PAGE 31
The *Duke of Aumale in the Courtyard of the Château in 1896*, photograph by Robert of Orléans, Duke of Chartres, Aumale's nephew.

Institut de France

Paris, le 24 Décembre 1886

Monseigneur et très honoré Confrère,

L'Institut de France, au moment où il vient d'accepter la donation que vous avez bien voulu lui faire de votre domaine de Chantilly, vous adresse l'expression de sa vive reconnaissance.

Par cette magnifique libéralité, vous n'avez pas seulement ajouté à l'éclat de notre institution, vous nous avez donné de puissants moyens d'aider au progrès des lettres, des sciences et des arts. Sans cesser d'être notre confrère, vous avez désormais votre place au premier rang des bienfaiteurs

À Monseigneur le Duc d'Aumale.

A Day with the Duke of Aumale

"Saturday, January 16. Today I begin my 76th year, having been born on January 16, 1822, in the Palais-Royal on rue de Valois. That morning my father had taken my great-aunt, the Duchess of Bourbon, to Dreux and he returned just in time to see me come into the world, at 9 p.m. Doctor at 8:30. Banned from hunting. Chantilly. Stroll through the Galleries. Work."

These are the words with which the Duke of Aumale described the last birthday he would celebrate, in his diary for 1897. He could be proud of what he had accomplished. He who had known exile and mourning, the dying glow of monarchy, the erratic start of the Third Republic, academic fame, and the excitement of collecting, seemed content. He had spent the last decades completing his life's work. He wanted to be a worthy heir to the age-old history of the château he had been given, restoring all its sparkle. "Wouldn't it be great luck today to own the home of the Connétable de Montmorency just as it existed in his day?" he wrote. "That's what I want to do with Chantilly." The Duke of Aumale's estate concretized the dream of a princely historian who wished to pay tribute to his glorious predecessors, Montmorency and Condé, as well as to his country's history.

He first asked Daumet to restore the Petit Château, built from 1557–58 onward by Jean Bullant for the king's chief officer, or *connétable,* Anne de Montmorency. Then Daumet turned, in 1875–80, to the main château, razed during the Revolution. Eclectic architecture was in fashion, so Chantilly, whose highly unusual plan respects historical layouts, is reminiscent of several major French Renaissance châteaux such as Amboise, Écouen, Chambord, Valençay, Fontainebleau, and Pau.

Set in extraordinary gardens, surrounded by abundant waters, and ringed by a vast forest conducive to hunting, this building was designed to house what is probably the most

amazing collection of the nineteenth century. But the château was also a home. It was populated by a small group of loyal servants who often became the museum's first guards. The prince's diaries describe the life he led. Mornings were often devoted to a trip to the stables and an outing on horseback. Then he would get down to work on the archives he had acquired on the Montmorency and Condé dynasties (in order to supplement his impressive *History of the Princes of Condé*). Or else he would pull a manuscript or drawing from his shelves. He could then unwind in one of the gardens he had restored: the seventeenth-century one designed by André Le Nôtre, the eighteenth-century "Anglo-Chinese" garden, or the landscape garden laid out early in the following century. Large receptions were regularly held in the evenings, as were lavish luncheons on Sundays, when Aumale liked to show his château to famous guests. An expert conversationalist, he would recount the history of his predecessors as he admired his treasures with his guests. ■

FACING PAGE
In the entrance, the statue of the Connétable de Montmorency, work of Paul Dubois.
BELOW
The Duke of Aumale's servants, prior to 1898. Notably included here are his gamekeepers, valets, and two bookbinders.

The Personal Lives of the Duke and Duchess of Aumale
The Private Apartments

The Private Apartments (*Petits Appartements*) were the result of the first major construction work carried out at Chantilly by the young Duke of Aumale. Having just married his cousin, Maria Carolina Augusta of Bourbon–Two Sicilies, in Naples in November 1844, he ordered that renovations begin in early 1845. The project was assigned to Eugène Lami, an interior decorator who also worked on the Palais des Tuileries, alongside architect Victor Dubois, who was quickly ousted, however. Lami and the duke came up with an interior in the latest fashion, full of references to the history of Chantilly while conducive to the installation of the ducal couple as the new owners of the premises. These apartments, endowed with all modern conveniences, were placed in the only surviving part of the château, the ground floor of the Renaissance wing.

The duchess's apartments were done in a lavishly feminine, eighteenth-century revival spirit. The antechamber, with white-and-gold woodwork like those in the upstairs rooms of the princes of Condé, combined Louis XV and Louis XVI styles. Called the Guise Salon (*Salon de Guise*), it is named after the title of the duke and duchess's younger son. The lavish furniture, mostly made by the Grohé brothers (as elsewhere in the apartments), was done in the same spirit. The bedroom next door is impressively theatrical—the duchess's monogram can be seen on the bedhead and fireplace mirror, as well as on a garland held by two parakeets painted on the ceiling by Narcisse Diaz. The room is dominated by a superb canopy bed reflecting the taste in fabrics of the day, accompanied by rosewood furniture and Louis XV style chairs that were given padded upholstery by Victor Cruchet. Souvenirs of the mistress of the house can be found everywhere—beneath the portrait

BACKGROUND IMAGE
Androuet du Cerceau, *Chantilly. Courtyard Façade with Annex Buildings*, copperplate engraving from the *Plus Excellens Bastimens de France* (detail), 1579.

FACING PAGE
Placed on the mantelpiece in the Purple Salon of the Duchess of Aumale's private apartments, a superb clock with a dial held by the Three Graces.

PAGES 38–39
The Purple Salon of the Duchess of Aumale's private apartments, where the interior, devised by Eugène Lami after the duke's return from exile, features silk satin fabrics whose purple hue indicates that the duke was mourning his deceased wife.

of the future Duchess of Aumale, painted by Schrotzberg when she was still living at the court of her uncle, the Emperor of Austria, is the magnificent cradle used for the couple's youngest son, François, Duke of Guise; it had been a present when he was born during the family's exile, in 1854. The pale blue satin on the walls has been reconstructed to correspond to the fabric ordered by the duke after his return from exile in 1876 (his wife had died in 1869), replacing a flowery white-and-pink wall fabric. The duchess's Gothic-revival prie-dieu (prayer stool)—which had graced her apartment in the Palais des Tuileries—evokes her devout piety, as do the various paintings of religious subjects and a small table (also used as a prie-dieu) decorated by Gabriele Capello with a tiny mosaic of Mount Etna erupting.

This row of rooms ends in a very modern bathroom and a round salon, or drawing room. The salon has a rich history, for it was formerly the bedroom of the Duchess of Bourbon, who gave birth in 1772 to the Duke of Enghien, the latest offspring of the Bourbon-Condé dynasty, whose bright future was cut short in 1804 when Napoleon had him executed in the moat of the château de Vincennes. Lami altered the shape of this room, endowing it with painted pilasters that imitated wood to match the rosewood furnishings, such as a *bureau à gradin* (small writing desk) and a Roller et Blanchet piano whose rounded back complements the rotundity of the room. Among the Louis XVI style chairs supplied by Alexis Ternisien are two original eighteenth-century chairs made by Jean-Baptiste Boulard in 1785 for the king's game room at Versailles; the latter were bought by Lami, who frequented the most important curio shops in Paris. The color of the satin upholstery—purple with a tone-on-tone scrollwork motif—may seem startling, but it was the color of mourning, and replaced the original, and probably worn, green upholstery when the newly widowed prince returned from exile.

This set of rooms includes one of Chantilly's treasures, namely a small mezzanine boudoir decorated in 1735 by animal painter Christophe Huet. Female monkeys gambol over the woodwork, dressed like Condé princesses and carrying out their favorite activities: lunching during a hunt, picking fruit, bathing, playing cards, skimming across frozen moats in sleds, and at their toilettes. This Petite Singerie—from the French for monkey, *singe*—is one of four surviving

FACING PAGE
Eighteenth-century-revival woodwork and mirror in the Guise Salon.
PAGES 42–43
The Guise Salon was named after the Duke and Duchess of Aumale's second son, whose portrait by Charles-François Jalabert can be seen here. This eighteenth-century-revival room served as an antechamber to the duchess's private apartments.

monkey décors in France, including the Grande Singerie, also at Chantilly. It reflects the Condé family's penchant for the Far East, monkeys being an animal closely associated with Asia. In addition to suggestive still lifes on the lower woodwork, the ceiling of this remarkably lavish and inventive setting also features scenes inspired by La Fontaine's *Fables* and depictions of the ordinary trades and crafts of Paris.

The row of rooms comprising the duke's apartment is more eclectic. His bedroom, paneled with woodwork partly from the eighteenth century, features overdoor paintings that evoke the history of Chantilly, done by Lami and his associates. The metal bed reflects Aumale's career as a general and his appreciation of austere military life. It contrasts with the lavish cylinder desk, made by the Grohé brothers in the Louis XV style, although the decorative medallion shows Louis XIV; King Louis-Philippe, who gave this desk to the duke, was thereby placing his son in an illustrious lineage. Near the bed is Aumale's death mask, as well as the tricolor flag that draped his coffin during its long procession from Sicily to Paris.

The drawing room next door, called the Condé Salon (*salon de Condé*), also evokes Louis XIV. The dominant feature is a fireplace imitating one in the château de Villeroy, with the addition of elegant bronze greyhounds sculpted by Antoine-Louis Barye. The walls are lined with crimson silk damask heightened by bands of lavish trimming. The Boulle or Boulle-revival furniture and the high-backed chairs upholstered in silk damask and velvet typify the seventeenth-century-revival interiors done by Lami for the Orléans family at the Palais des Tuileries. This drawing room hosted the desk at which the Duke of Aumale worked, surrounded by the Condé princes ranging from the Grand Condé to the duke's godfather, the Duke of Bourbon; the medallions by Jean-Marie Ribou, from the late eighteenth century, depict nobles of the Houses of Bourbon and Bourbon-Condé.

We then move to the marble dining room (*chambre de Marbre*), which is Renaissance in feel, oscillating between the styles of Henri II and Henri IV. The walls are lined in blue wool. Over the Henri IV fireplace are weapons and armor dating from the sixteenth century. The furniture, notably the showcase-dresser made by the Grohé brothers, alludes to the decorative idiom of the château de Fontainebleau, whereas the marble flooring was based on a portrait of King Henri IV painted

FACING PAGE
The Duchess of Aumale's
bedroom, featuring a canopy
bed in the grand eighteenth-
century tradition.

ABOVE
This cradle was a gift from
Madame de Vatry, the owner
of the nearby Chaalis Abbey,
upon the birth of François,
Duke of Guise, in 1856.

"The year begins with a fine day; the weather is mild and clear; the delightful appearance of this handsome place only increases my melancholy; I look at the pictures of the three beloved beings I have lost, and I feel the full weight of sadness, of my loneliness. The future seems dark and uncertain."

Diary of the Duke of Aumale, January 1, 1873

FACING PAGE
This so-called Hungarian toiletry set was a wedding gift to the Duke and Duchess of Aumale upon their marriage in November 1844.

PAGES 50–51
The Petite Singerie, painted by Christophe Huet in 1735, is the only eighteenth-century room in the private apartments to have remained intact during renovation work in 1845–47.

by Frans Pourbus (now in the Louvre), as Lami himself noted (he liked to make specific, richly symbolic allusions). Indeed, the Duke of Aumale's first name, Henri, came from the first Bourbon king, Henri IV.

A gallery with Renaissance-revival woodwork was built in 1847 by a promising young architect, Félix Duban, who would go on to restore the château de Blois. This gallery offered discreet access to the row of rooms without entering the main rooms. It was done in a style and materials that pay tribute to Bullant's stone architecture while making its own

statement. Display cases with the coat of arms of all the previous owners of Chantilly further united the entire history of the premises under the aegis of their new owner.

That history was tinged with sorrow. After returning from exile, the Duke of Aumale created a veritable memorial to his family. He arrayed souvenirs of the dear departed—his parents, brothers, sisters, and his two sons, who died aged eighteen and twenty-one. Drawn, painted, and sculpted portraits, as well as photographs, evoke the pain of a man who no longer wanted to occupy these rooms—except at the very end of his life. Here, in what he called his "cemetery," a gloomy, inconsolable Henri of Orléans would sometimes sink into a dark reverie, as suggested by a few lines entered in his diary on January 1, 1873. "Chantilly. The year begins with a fine day; the weather is mild and clear; the delightful appearance of this handsome place only increases my melancholy; I look at the pictures of the three beloved beings I have lost, and I feel the full weight of sadness, of my loneliness. The future seems dark and uncertain."

Yet it was ultimately this tragedy-filled history that resulted in the unique, almost complete, preservation of these apartments in their 1840s state: the duke wanted to retain the atmosphere of those happy years, prior to the revolution of 1848 and his long exile in England. These private apartments are in fact France's only completely preserved princely dwelling from the period known as the July Monarchy (1830–48). By harking back to the days of Chantilly's splendor from the sixteenth to eighteenth centuries, they constitute a unique record of the history of grand French interiors, all the while being forerunners of the comfortable revival style known as "Second Empire" (1852–70), which in fact emerged—notably right here—between 1845 and 1847. ∎

FACING PAGE
The Condé Salon is decorated in a Louis XIV style harking back to the days of the Grand Condé, seen standing in front of the Battle of Rocroi in this portrait by Juste d'Egmont, c. 1655.

PAGES 58–59
The marble-floored chamber that formerly served as the dining room of the private apartments was decorated in a Renaissance-revival style. The furnishings by the Grohé brothers were inspired by the school of Fontainebleau.

BOURBON-CONDÉ
(LOUIS II, LE GRAND)
1621–1686

132

The Last Holy Chapel in the History of France

The chapel, with a steeple rising above the château, was built by Daumet between 1875 and 1885. In one final echo of the Sainte-Chapelle in Paris, this chapel's silhouette is worthy of the finest illuminated manuscript, the *Très Riches Heures du Duc de Berry*. For that matter, the chapel is dedicated to Saint Louis—or King Louis IX, who built the Sainte-Chapelle—seen holding the crown of thorns in the statue by Marqueste above the façade. This is a chapel for a prince of the blood, a descendent of Saint Louis, proclaiming his rank and paying homage to his predecessors.

Indeed, the Duke of Aumale designed a veritable mausoleum inspired by major examples of French Renaissance architecture, notably the chapel of the château d'Écouen. He wanted to recreate the chapel of the famous Connétable de Montmorency by displaying Renaissance artworks from the Montmorency château in Écouen, which the Condés had recovered during the Bourbon Restoration (1815) and which the duke had subsequently inherited. Below a heraldic vault evoking Aumale's princely and royal ancestry, as well as the rallying cries of French armies during the ancien régime, the altar is decorated with the Connétable's emblems. The altarpiece, depicting the sacrifice of Isaac, reflects the classical inspiration of mid-sixteenth-century art. All around are twelve panels showing Christ's apostles in a setting worthy of a grand royal chapel, within partly modified woodwork bearing the emblem of Henri II (making it possible to date it to 1548). The stained glass, dated 1544, shows the sons and daughters of Montmorency, and was set by artist Edmond Lechevallier-Chevignard in large nineteenth-century windows; the children are accompanied by their father, Anne de Montmorency, and mother, Madeleine de Savoie, painted by Dominique Henri Guifard from cartoons designed by Lechevallier-Chevignard in 1889.

BACKGROUND IMAGE
Androuet du Cerceau, *Chantilly. Courtyard Façades* (detail).

FACING PAGE
View of the chapel, with a Renaissance-revival décor that matches the sixteenth-century works originally from the chapel of the château d'Écouen.

PAGES 62–63
The monument designed to house the hearts of the princes of Condé, sculpted by Jacques Sarrazin in the mid-seventeenth century. Their hearts are still entombed there.

Behind the Montmorency memorial is the Bourbon-Condé necropolis. Following the round plan of the old castle tower in which that family lived, this chapel behind the altar houses a monument containing the hearts of the Condés, placed there in 1885. The six statues and bas-reliefs on the monument are by Jacques Sarazin, one of the most important French sculptors of the mid-seventeenth century. From left to right we see allegorical figures of Justice (with sword and scales), Religion (with putto and stork), Prudence (in the guise of Minerva), and Piety (hands crossed on her chest), plus two children holding a shield. The bas-reliefs depict the Triumphs of Death, Time, Fame, and Eternity. The monument, commissioned in 1648 by the Grand Condé to hold the heart of his father, was originally placed in the Jesuit church of Saint-Paul-Saint-Louis in Paris. The urn in the middle contains the embalmed hearts of Condé princes down to the Duke of Aumale's elder son, who died in Sydney in 1866. ■

FACING PAGE
The stained glass showing
the sons of the Connétable de
Montmorency (detail), 1544.

A Palace for Horses

Aged barely ten, the Duke of Aumale already expressed amazement at the monumentality and magnificence of the Chantilly stables in a letter to his sister Louise, Queen of the Belgians. "We went to see the stables, which astonished me: it is a magnificent building of remarkable solidity." Right to the end of his life, the duke, an eminent horseman, would go to this veritable palace for horses to see his favorite steeds—first Baba-Ali, then Pélagie—which he rode on outings or for hunting.

The stables, so huge that they are sometimes mistaken for the château itself, were the dream of one of his predecessors, Louis Henri, Prince of Condé. That ambitious prince, named prime minister to the young Louis XV in 1723, became rich through John Law's speculative economic scheme, only to be disgraced in 1726, when he withdrew to his property. It hardly mattered, for at Chantilly he would leave his mark, pursuing the incredible plan of building majestic stables that reflected his prestige and embodied his passion for riding and hunting.

Work, which had begun in 1719, came to an end in 1735, although still incomplete. Architect Jean Aubert, who had trained under Jules Hardouin-Mansart, designed the complex as well as the princely apartments he was building at the château. Aubert was greatly inspired by the large and small stables at Versailles, built by his mentor—and he managed to outdo both. The Grand Stables (*Grandes Écuries*) at Chantilly, among the largest in Europe, mark a high point in equestrian culture. Located at the edge of a forest full of game, they set the stage for that aristocratic pastime par excellence, hunting.

Their ingenious layout reflects the various roles they played. There are several points of entry and several perspectives. The stables established an initial axis that visually ran in a line from one of the stately rooms in the château, the Corner

FACING PAGE
A view of the Grand Stables and Jeu de Paume in the eighteenth century.

Room (*Cabinet d'Angle*), being built at that same time by Aubert for Prince Louis Henri. This axis continued along the façade of the stables, some 600 feet (182 meters) in length, facing a lawn and the woods. Flanking a central pavilion were two tall wings that could house as many as 240 horses—in 1740 there were 220. These architectural masterpieces, based on the Orangery in Versailles designed by Hardouin-Mansart, had vaults of rounded arches that flaunted perfect stonecutting technique. The bare stone had no need of ornamentation, apart from the light that played across the pale limestone drawn from a quarry beneath the current race track. The central pavilion boasts a monumental dome 85 feet (25 meters) high, sheltering an indoor riding ring that served as the main entrance, the point of departure and return from the hunt. Behind, three courtyards flanked a church dedicated to Our Lady of the Assumption, built somewhat earlier to a design by Hardouin-Mansart; they hosted an outdoor ring, outbuildings that housed the carriages, saddlery, and smithy, as well as kennels for hunting hounds that numbered in the hundreds. Two pavilions flank the entrance to this outer ring—one opened into the main wings, while the other, never completed (known today as Porte Saint-Denis), led toward the town, which was literally built in line with the stables.

Whereas the outer walls feature linear rustication orchestrated around pilasters and columns—in the tradition of the stables at Versailles—the upper sections of this equestrian palace boast opulent rococo decoration that reflects the hierarchy and purposes of the various spaces. Thus the entrance to the outer ring is marked by the coat of arms of the prince who commissioned it, framed by two majestically rearing horses. The entrance to the central pavilion, meanwhile, crowned by a 1989 reconstruction of the statue of Fame, has a tympanum with three snorting horses, who are seen again on the tympana over the doors to the southeast and southwest pavilions. The entrance to the kennels, on the other hand, features a hunting theme. Even the oculi, or round windows, on the central dome boast thoroughly rococo decoration both inside and out; the abundant, lively ornamentation was carved in the 1730s by Rémy François Bridault and his assistants Coutelet, Brault, Lefèvre, and Bernard.

"[The stables] are magnificent: the exterior looks like a palace, the interior surprises and amazes…. It's hard to believe that such a beautiful building was erected to house horses. Ancien-régime monks in their refectory were arrayed with no less order nor served with no less precision and care than were the former prince's horses at Chantilly."

Louis Damin, *Le Voyageur Curieux et Sentimental*, 1796

The northeast pavilion, where only the façade was built, bears witness to the halt to this extraordinary dream. As the focus of an entire society devoted to riding and hunting, with dozens of stable officers and kennels, these stables were not only a functional building with a skillful, rational layout, but also—and above all—a mark of power. Geographically distant from Versailles, yet very close in ambition and inspiration, the stables at Chantilly were the triumphant setting of incredible festivities throughout the eighteenth century.

Fortunately, they survived Revolutionary demolition, and during the First Empire (1804–15) the stables housed Napoleon's Polish light cavalry regiments. At the Restoration, the Bourbons returned them to their original use and restored the hunting facilities.

In the 1830s, when the young Duke of Aumale became the new proprietor, another role for the stables emerged—one with a brilliant future. The quality of the lawn in front of them was conducive to the development of "English racing" promoted by the duke's older brother, Ferdinand-Philippe of Orléans, who invested in the creation of a racetrack and the establishment of prizes. The first race was held here on May 15, 1834. The Duke of Aumale set up his own stable in turn, and followed his brother into racing. Upon his return from exile, major restorations were carried out, with newer, larger stalls and boxes. After the duke died, his equestrian statue was placed here in 1899, based on a design by artist Jean Léon Gérôme and funded by the citizens of Chantilly through subscription.

In the mid-twentieth century the Grand Stables were the preserve of a few privileged horsemen and women—members of the Cercle hippique—but were opened to the public in 1982 thanks to Yves Benaimé, who founded the Living Horse Museum (*Musée Vivant du Cheval*). They have been managed since 2005 by the Fondation pour la Sauvegarde et le Développement du Domaine de Chantilly, which ensures the restoration and valorization of premises that continue to house horses while perpetuating the tradition of haute-école equestrianism. ∎

"The stable, with its wonderful lawn, is ridiculously beautiful—finer than any château."

Journal du Duc de Croÿ (1718–1784)

ABOVE
Pierre Vernet, *Horse Races
at Chantilly in May 1836*, 1836.
PAGES 80–81
The entrance to the riding ring
and the Porte Saint-Denis.

A Hunting Estate

The Duke of Aumale's library held an original edition of the *Livre du Roi Modus et de la Reine Ratio* (Book of King Method and Queen Theory), printed at Chambéry in 1486. The text, written by Henri de Ferrières in the second half of the fourteenth century, had been highly popular in manuscript form. This volume was thus the first printed version of a famous huntbook devoted to venery, falconry, and archery. The aristocratic pastime of hunting also inspired the arts: at Chantilly, for instance, a sculpted pack of hounds welcomes visitors, the Stag Gallery (*Galerie des Cerfs*) features hunt-themed decoration, and a picture by Eugène Fromentin in the Gallery of Painting depicts *Heron Hunting*, constantly reminding us that Aumale was an enthusiastic fan of various types of hunting.

In the nineteenth century, hunting with hounds was a sport that, more than any other, had its customs and parlance. It was also the pastime of an elite that liked to get together and discuss rivalries between "fields," who wore color-coded riding garments with decorative buttons of symbolic significance. The Duke of Aumale liked to ride, which he did every morning until he was very old. Ever since the Middle Ages, the hunt has been an ideal activity for soldiers when not at war. Aumale was keen to maintain, for his own prestige, the reputation of the Condé princes as great hunters. His guests at memorable hunts included the Prince of Wales (the future Edward VII), Empress Elisabeth of Austria ("Sissi," a great rider), Archduke Vladimir of Russia, and members of old ducal families as well as nouveaux riches. He posed for a portrait by Lami in hunting dress worthy of Louis XV, with his horn on his shoulder. Lami also did a portrait of the duke on Baba-Ali, his steed in Algeria. Aumale liked to be surrounded by grooms and stable boys who constituted a club of excellent professionals. They took care

FACING PAGE
Auguste Nicolas Cain, *Hunting Hounds* (detail), 1880. The two depicted here in bronze were called Fanfaraut and Brillador.

of his thirty-two horses and his pack of hounds—each dog was branded with the heraldic mark of cadency that the Condés, as a younger branch of the royal family, added to the coat of arms of France. On the arrival of the duke, the hornsmen would sound his personal fanfare, as well as those of his illustrious guests. By tradition, stags and roebucks were hunted at Chantilly. When exiled in 1886, the duke had to sell his horses, but he reassembled his stable when he returned to France. When too old for such games, he passed the torch to his nephew, the Duke of Chartres (son of his brother, the Duke of Orléans). Dressed in blue colors, and with as much panache as his uncle, the Duke of Chartres maintained the hunt at Chantilly until his death in 1910. ■

BELOW
Chantilly: Château and Stag-Hunting Party, photograph by Robert of Orléans.

FACING PAGE
The billiards room, called the King's Salon, in the lower level of the Grand Château, is adorned with a bust of King Louis-Philippe and stags' antlers.

PAGE 86
The Daumet gallery that once led to guest rooms has been transformed into the museum's department of prints and drawings.

PAGE 87
Auguste Nicolas Cain, *Seated Stag* (detail), 1890.

ABOVE
Eugène Lami, *Portrait of
the Duke of Aumale
in Hunting Attire*, 1845.
Musée de la Vénerie, Senlis.

FACING PAGE
The main hall leading to the
Grand Apartments, overlooked
by a bust of King Henri IV,
founder of the French Bourbon
dynasty, after whom the Duke of
Aumale was named. Flanking
the door are busts of the duke's
godfather and godmother, the
Duke of Bourbon and Madame
Adélaïde (sister of King
Louis-Philippe).

DE BON ROY, BON HEVR

"It is not expressed clearly, but is mingled amongst the words, like the morning mist at Chantilly."

Marcel Proust, *Contre Sainte-Beuve*

FACING PAGE
The hunting theme dominates
the Antechamber, notably thanks
to paintings by Jean-Baptiste Oudry
and François Desportes, inherited
from the princes of Condé.

PAGE 92
Victor Mottez, *Portrait of the Duke
of Aumale at Claremont*, 1853.

PAGE 93
The Duchess of Aumale on Horseback,
photograph by W. T. Deane.

PAGES 94–95
Jean-Maxime Claude, *The Hounds
Leaving the Grand Stables
at Chantilly*, 1865.

The Grand Apartments
Condé Splendor

In the Grand Apartments (*Grands Appartements*), the Duke of Aumale could literally walk in his predecessors' footsteps. He enjoyed regaling his guests with stories of the Condés' fame. "The rest of us talk, but he speaks," said writer and philosopher Ernest Renan, who, like the duke, was a member of the Académie Française. Beyond the Antechamber with its hunt-themed decoration (including two paintings commissioned in 1724 by Louis Henri de Bourbon-Condé from Jean-Baptiste Oudry), the Guard Room (*Salle des Gardes*) is devoted to the military arts. There reigns a portrait of the Grand Condé by Juste d'Egmont. Display cases exhibit items related to the Condé army (a counter-revolutionary force headed by French princes) and to the Duke of Aumale's campaigns in Algeria during the July Monarchy. The fireplace mantle, meanwhile, features an ancient mosaic of the *Abduction of Europa* (first century CE) from the Villa San Marco, buried when Mount Vesuvius erupted. Both rooms were revamped by Honoré Daumet to connect the Grand Château to the Petit Château. Then come the eighteenth-century apartments of the princes of Condé. Their current layout in the Petit Château was designed during the Renaissance by Hardouin-Mansart toward the end of the Grand Condé's life, but ever since being renovated around 1720 they have constituted one of the most coherent, important examples of early rococo decoration in France.

The princes' ceremonial bedchamber, where an alcove bed was located prior to the Revolution, is adorned with five large canvases done in 1735 by animal painter Christophe Huet, but only placed there after the Restoration. The woodwork, done in 1720–25 under the supervision of Jean Aubert by decorative artist Charles Louis Maurisan and gilders Autin and Désauzières, reflects the transition from Louis XIV to Louis XV style. Subtle ornamental variations of shells, ivy, trelliswork, trophies, dogs, dragons, and quivers extend from the bedchamber to the Music Room (*Salon de Musique*) via the Corner Room (*Cabinet d'Angle*), Grande Singerie, and Battle Gallery (*Galerie des Batailles*). ∎

BACKGROUND IMAGE
Androuet du Cerceau, *Chantilly. Courtyard Façades* (detail), 1579.

FACING PAGE
Detail of rococo woodwork in the Grand Apartments.

A COLLECTION OF
HISTORIC FURNITURE

Aware of his status and the new luster he had to bring to Chantilly and its interiors, the Duke of Aumale bought marvelous furnishings and objets d'art. Although not as obsessed by French eighteenth-century decorative art as the likes of James de Rothschild, the Marquess of Hertford, or Moïse de Camondo, the duke could be very proud of the collection he assembled.

Yet this taste was not inherited: his father, Louis-Philippe, mainly favored the Empire style, while his godfather, the last prince of Condé, preferred elegant but unfussy Restoration furniture by Jacob-Desmalter, Marcion, and Bellangé.

The fabulous items found at Chantilly prior to the Revolution were confiscated or sold; when the Condé princes returned from exile during the Restoration, they demanded restitution of their treasures, but obtained only a few proud items that now preside at Chantilly like witnesses of bygone days. They include one piece of furniture that encapsulates the scientific and artistic ambitions of the Enlightenment as well as the diplomatic relations between nobles of that day: a cabinet given by King Gustav III of Sweden to Louis Joseph de Bourbon-Condé after a stay at Chantilly that made a strong impression on the king. It was made in 1774 by Swedish furniture-maker Georg Haupt, and its function is inscribed in its decorative marquetry and top—the twenty-seven little drawers were designed to hold the Condés' collection of semi-precious stones and minerals. The cabinet's overall lines and decoration reflect the neoclassical fashion that arose in France in the middle of the eighteenth century.

FACING PAGE
The gem and mineral cabinet made by
Georg Haupt, given by King Gustav III of
Sweden to Louis Joseph of Bourbon-
Condé in 1774.

Once the Duke of Aumale took actual possession of the château following his marriage, he hired Lami to refurbish the Grand Apartments as well as the Private Apartments. He gave free rein to the eclecticism then in fashion, with an emphasis on an eighteenth-century style that accorded with the interior decoration. He commissioned the Grohé brothers to make Boulle-revival stands for busts of the Grand Condé and Turenne to go with the Boulle table in the Battle Gallery. He also used glamorous furnishings from the Condé château at Écouen, such as the so-called vine table, the oldest piece of furniture at Chantilly (c. 1540), which bears the motto of Connétable Anne de Montmorency. In the Corner Room, Louis XVI chairs by Jean-Baptiste Sené cozy up to an imposing central post crowned by a large Louis XIV style dish decorated with a bronze bas-relief of the battle of the Amazons, after Rubens, made by the Marrel brothers, as a gift from Queen Maria Amelia to her son in 1847.

The Duke of Aumale constantly added to this glamorous collection. When his father's estate was auctioned in 1857, he bought remarkable pieces of furniture that came from his grandmother, the Dowager Duchess of Orléans, who had bought the furnished home of imperial chancellor Jean-Jacques Régis de Cambacérès. It included what is probably the Musée Condé's most notable piece of furniture: a commode (chest of drawers) from Louis XVI's bedroom at Versailles, now in the bedchamber of the princes of Condé. Made by the great cabinetmaker Jean-Henri Riesener in 1775, its neoclassical monumentality glorifies royal authority. Four impressive bronze caryatids representing Mars, Hercules, Temperance, and Prudence seem to be holding up the marble top. It is an exceptional item of furniture thanks to the harmony of its chased, gilded bronzework and inlay of

FACING PAGE
The commode by Jean-Henri Riesener,
now in the Prince's Chamber,
originally came from Louis XVI's
bedroom in Versailles.
PAGES 102–3
The front panel of the commode from
Louis XVI's bedroom (detail).

nine different kinds of wood (the mosaic decoration of rosettes and central panel with a rustic theme was altered by the cabinetmaker in 1794 to eliminate all monarchist decoration). It enters into a dialogue with another Riesener commode, made for the director of the royal furniture depository, Pierre de Fontanieu. Almost every room at Chantilly boasts some piece of furniture with a royal provenance.

In 1882, during the famous sale of property belonging to his friend the Duke of Hamilton, Aumale bought two eighteenth-century filing desks, the first made around 1770 for the Duke of Choiseul, attributed to Œben, and the second for Lalive de Jully, who introduced ambassadors to the French court at Versailles and was a forward-looking collector. This latter desk, attributed to Joseph Baumhauer, is a harbinger of French neoclassicism in so far as it contains all the seeds of the "Greek" style. Its masculine, almost martial look must have pleased General of Aumale, while its style and the unprecedented quality of its bronzes make it a benchmark in the history of furniture.

Yet Chantilly, simultaneously a museum and a home, also had to be furnished comfortably. Hence display cases, bookshelves, desks, and chairs of all kinds, often made by the duke's favorite cabinetmaker, Guillaume Grohé, provided a real context for living as well as collecting. ∎

FACING PAGE
Detail of the gilt-bronze
decoration on the large dish made by
the Marrel brothers in 1847.
PAGES 106–7
Filing desk made for Ange Laurent Lalive de Jully,
attributed to Joseph Baumhauer (detail).

CHANTILLY SOFT-PASTE PORCELAIN

Long before Sèvres, Chantilly hosted one of the most creative porcelain manufactories of the eighteenth century. The secret behind porcelain, known in China since the ninth century, became an obsession of Enlightenment Europe, which sought to discover it by all means. That notably included Louis Henri, Prince of Condé, an eminent collector of Asian porcelain, who wanted to set up his own manufactory, a key mark of prestige. He turned to porcelain-maker Ciquaire Cirou, who from 1730 onward developed a workshop in Chantilly to make soft-paste porcelain ("soft," and therefore more fragile, because lacking kaolin, the white clay that is the raw material of true Chinese porcelain). In 1735 the prince obtained a royal warrant authorizing him to make Japanese-style porcelain. Thus up to the 1750s Chantilly specialized in "Kakiemon" ware, composed of Japanese-style designs in a limited palette of colors on a white ground. This style matched the craze for chinoiserie, that is to say fascination with the aesthetics of the Far East. The Prince of Condé supplied the workshop with Asian porcelain from his own collection to serve as models for the potters, who turned out extravagant tea services and amusing figurines of animals as well as imaginary Chinese creatures. By the mid-eighteenth century, Chantilly began adopting more European shapes and styles—rococo or naturalistic—featuring flowers and insects in a broader range of colors, all the while turning out table services on a wider scale. But the growing number of exclusive privileges accorded to the Sèvres manufactory soon restricted the use of gold and colors at Chantilly. The workshop then began specializing in white and blue table services decorated with a "sprig" or carnation pattern. It carried on until the French Revolution, when it lost the patronage of the princes of Condé. The manufactory was nevertheless bought by an Englishman, Christopher Potter, and survived until 1870, even though it had lost its ancien-régime dynamism. ■

THE GRANDE SINGERIE

One of the most refined rooms in the château is called the Grande Singerie, *singe* being French for "monkey." Monkeys were an exotic animal par excellence, associated in the eighteenth century with the Far East. They frequently featured in chinoiserie, so beloved by Louis Henri de Bourbon-Condé, who commissioned the decoration of this room. He called upon Christophe Huet, who trained under Claude III Audran and was an animal painter specializing in singeries. (He did similar rooms in the Rohan residence in Paris and the château de Champs-sur-Marne.) Huet also did a fire screen bought by the Duke of Aumale. Two years after having painted the Petite Singerie at Chantilly, he decorated the larger Grande Singerie—the date 1737 can be seen carved on a block of marble by a monkey-sculptor. Abundant, gleeful imagery covers the room from floor to ceiling, showing a fanciful China where monkeys exist alongside amusing little figures in Chinese-style dress. Themes and interpretations are woven across six panels, three double-leaf doors, and the ceiling. There are images that evoke the five senses: monkey-musicians appeal to hearing; touch is suggested by the panel where a woman is being handed a letter as well as the forepaw of a hunted prey; a little fellow on a hammock, surrounded by monkeys with a teapot and a chocolate pot, alludes to taste; vision, meanwhile, is represented by an alchemist admiring his collection of paintings and porcelain; and smell is symbolized by monkeys burning incense before a fine lady. The four corners of the earth are also represented: four grisaille medallions

flanking the two mirrors show animals traditionally associated with the four known continents—crocodile, elephant, horse, and lion. The four large panels at the end of the room allude to these same continents: the woman being offered a forepaw wears a headdress with feathers associated with America; the pale woman graced with incense is Europe; the alchemist represents Africa; and the lounging gentleman, Asia. To the left of the fireplace, one of the most interesting panels evokes the princes of Condé and life at Chantilly: an alchemist surrounded by jars, in front of a painting, is next to a monkey decorating pottery, while another paints arabesques. The alchemist wittily alludes to the man who commissioned this extraordinary décor, shown among all the products of the manufactories he established, as well as his famous cabinet of natural history, suggested by the jars and retorts. Furthermore, alchemy recalls the prince's interest in porcelain (whose secret was being sought at the time), as well as his personal enrichment thanks to economist John Law, the famous inventor of paper money who ultimately went resoundingly bankrupt, perhaps symbolized here by the thrifty squirrel bent over a press, printing banknotes. The multiple meanings of all this imagery extend to allegories of the arts and sciences (war, painting, hunting, music, geography, sculpture, geometry, chemistry, and alchemy), all the while depicting princely pastimes—monkeys dressed in the purple-and-buff Bourbon-Condé livery conduct various kinds of hunt. ∎

FACING PAGE
A panel in the Grande Singerie
showing a fanciful figure in Chinese-style
dress in a hammock, playing music,
and two monkeys.

The Battle Gallery

The Duke of Aumale enjoyed recounting the military exploits of Louis II of Bourbon, Prince of Condé, known as the Grand Condé, when showing his guests the gallery dubbed The Deeds of the Prince (*Les Actions de Monsieur le Prince*), also called the Battle Gallery (*Galerie des Batailles*). The gallery was built by architect Jules Hardouin-Mansart toward the end of the Grand Condé's life, along with the rest of the Grand Apartments. As in the Hall of Mirrors at Versailles, panels of woodwork alternate with large mirrors that reflect the light from six windows, adding glitter to the gilding. The woodwork was redone around 1720 in a more fashionable taste; the cornice, adorned with a series of military trophies and musical instruments, accompanied by the little cherubs known as putti, emphasizes the martial theme of this gallery, whose main goal is to depict the Grand Condé's victories. Between 1687 and 1694 Sauveur Le Conte, an artist who trained under Van der Meulen and specialized in battle scenes, delivered eleven paintings of the Grand Condé's victorious campaigns. They all followed a similar composition: the battle in the center—the main event—is surrounded by medallions illustrating other clashes; the Grand Condé is systematically shown in a commanding pose. It is his fame—hence the fame of his family—that is being underscored here.

His military career unfolds in a clockwise direction. The first painting, *The Battle of Rocroi*, shows the 1643 battle in which Condé saved France from Spanish invasion during the Thirty Years War, shortly after the death of Louis XIII, when the young Louis XIV was only five years old. There follow the German campaigns, then the conflicts in the first phase of the civil war known as the Fronde (1648–49), when Condé commanded the royal armies on behalf of the king and Cardinal Mazarin. The cycle ends with campaigns carried out under Louis XIV, notably *Crossing the Rhine*, the 1672 battle in which Condé was wounded for the only time—his wrist was

BACKGROUND IMAGE
Androuet du Cerceau,
Chantilly. Courtyard Façades
(detail), 1579.
FACING PAGE
Bust of the Grand Condé,
attributed to Antoine Coysevox.
PAGES 118–19
The Battle Gallery.
PAGES 120–21
Sauveur Le Conte,
*The Battle of Rocroi and
the Campaign of 1643.*

L'ELEVATION DE
THIONVILLE.

LA CARTE DV GOVVERNEMENT
DE THIONVILLE.

LE SIEGE DE THIONVILLE

BA
ROCH
ENTRE L'ARMÉE D
MONSEIGNEVR
CELLE DV ROY D
PAR DOM FR

LORDRE

LA
E DE
ONNEE
MAY 1643
Y COMMANDÉS PAR
C D'ANGVIEN ET
GNE COMMANDÉE
ISCO DE MELLO

L'ELEVATION
DE SIRCK.

LA CARTE DV GOVVERNEMENT
DE SIRCK.

LE SIEGE DE SIRCK

TAILLE

shattered by a pistol shot—and in which his nephew, Charles-Paris of Orléans-Longueville, was killed. This is also the only painting to show the king, on horseback in the center, with Condé humbly placed behind his monarch.

In the middle of the gallery, hanging between the blockade of Paris (in 1649) and the conquest of Franche-Comté (in 1668), is a painting that is entirely different in composition. Done by Michel II Corneille at the request of the Grand Condé's son, it is an allegorical depiction of "the prince's repentance": the Grand Condé, dressed like a Roman emperor, prevents Fame from singing the praises of his victorious battles against the armies of his cousin, King Louis XIV, during the second phase of the Fronde (1652–59). On the contrary, he orders Fame to trumpet his repentance even as his foot crushes the names of his victories over the French royal armies (names that nevertheless remain legible, as are the pages of the book torn out by Clio, the muse of History, leaning on Time, personified by Saturn with his scythe and hourglass). Although the Grand Condé thus wished to remove these victories from posterity, his repentance was extremely clever: although with apparent regret, it clearly records his exploits. ■

BELOW
Ancient view of the Battle Gallery.
FACING PAGE
Michel II Corneille, *The Grand Condé's Repentance*, 1692. The Grand Condé asks that his repentance for opposing King Louis XIV be trumpeted, while Clio, the muse of history, tears from the records the pages recounting his victories over the king.

OVANTVM POENITVIT

PRIS

St GVLAIN

THE GRAND CONDÉ:
A MODEL FIGURE

The Battle Gallery is a memorial to the Grand Condé. The Duke of Aumale identified closely with Condé, for as a young and brilliant General Aumale captured the main camp (or *smalah*) of Abdelkader in Algeria in May 1843, nearly two hundred years, to the day, after Condé's resounding victory at Rocroi. The duke also underwent exile, like Condé, and again like the prince was a grand patron of Chantilly. In the middle of the gallery he installed a display case dedicated to his hero, whose biography he had written. Here are shown Condé's purported weapons and banners, as well as portraits—a painting by Jacques Stella and a sculpture by Antoine Coysevox. The prince's marble bust has its pendant, opposite, in a bust of his cousin and rival, the Viscount of Turenne. These, the two greatest military leaders of the seventeenth century, were both great-grandsons of the famous Connétable de Montmorency, who built this wing of the château de Chantilly. On the fireplace, statuettes in bisque and terracotta show the Grand Condé at the battle of Freiburg, throwing his marshal's baton into enemy lines in order to spur his troops to follow him in recovering it. When gazing at all these depictions, the Duke of Aumale inevitably recounted his predecessor's victories in great detail. ∎

FACING PAGE
Jacques Stella, *Louis II of Bourbon, Duke of Enghien*. The future Grand Condé is shown in festive dress.

The Stag Gallery
The Art of Hospitality

The central location and size of the dining room, called the Stag Gallery (*Galerie des Cerfs*), demonstrate that Chantilly was designed to receive guests, in British-style comfort. That is where the Duke of Aumale hosted Sunday lunches for the elite of the day, ranging from crowned heads (like Austrian Empress Sissi), to writers (Alexandre Dumas fils, Émile Zola, Pierre Loti), painters, fellow academicians, military leaders, and, of course, his family. Although people barely listened to the musicians playing in the gallery over the doorway, they liked to hear the duke recount his stories—indeed, history. They were dazzled. "What they like best," wrote Paul Lippmann in *Le Monde Moderne* in November 1895, "is to let their august host talk throughout the meal. He, meanwhile, takes no greater pleasure, when he feels he is among his close friends and former comrades in arms, than in telling them about the château made famous by his ancestors."

The decoration of the room gave free rein to his passion for history. The high coffered ceiling—in Renaissance style in tribute to the Connétable de Montmorency, and similar to the one in the ballroom at Fontainebleau (where Henri IV also installed a Stag Gallery)—is adorned with the coats of arms of all the owners of Chantilly. It also resembles the dining room in the château de Pau, restored by the duke's father, King Louis-Philippe. At both Pau and Chantilly the walls are lined with tapestries depicting the Hunts of Maximilian, woven at Les Gobelins. Here we have the version woven from Van Orley's designs for the Count of Toulouse, an illegitimate son of Louis XIV, who was one of Aumale's forebears. The duke bought these treasures at the auction of his father Louis-Philippe's estate.

FACING PAGE
Decorative details of the Stag Gallery.

The bronze gas lamps inspired Jean Cocteau when designing the set of his 1946 film, *Beauty and the Beast*. The château de Chantilly was one of the first residences to be lit by gas in the late nineteenth century. In this enchanting setting, meals were still partly served in the old traditional French style, with several courses placed at once on the vast table, some forty feet (twelve meters) long. The dishes were prepared in the pantry next door, sometimes accompanied by the famous zucco, a sweet wine made in the duke's Sicilian vineyard. Once the ladies had withdrawn to avoid the smoke, the gentlemen could finally enjoy cigars with their coffee and liqueurs in the Gallery of Painting (*Galerie de Peinture*). ■

"What they like best is to let their august host talk throughout the meal. He, meanwhile, takes no greater pleasure, when he feels he is among his close friends and former comrades in arms, than in telling them about the château made famous by his ancestors."

Paul Lippmann, *Le Monde Moderne*, November 1895

VATEL:
LEGEND VERSUS
HISTORY

"Vatel, the great Vatel, late maître-d'hôtel to Monsieur Fouquet, and [now] in that capacity with the Prince, a man so eminently distinguished for taste, and whose abilities were equal to the government of a state—this man, whom I knew so well, finding, at eight o'clock this morning, that the fish he had sent for did not come at the time he expected it, and unable to bear the disgrace that he thought would inevitably attach to him, ran himself through with his own sword." This letter, written by Madame de Sévigné to her daughter on April 24, 1671, is the source of the legend surrounding François Vatel.

Originally from Picardy, Vatel first served as majordomo to Nicolas Fouquet, Louis XIV's superintendent of finances. His job was extremely important, for he was charged with ensuring supplies, organizing moves, and also transporting furniture and tableware. His talents were so great that government ministers like Colbert and Mazarin—and even Louis XIV himself—had called upon his services. It was Vatel who organized the lavish festivities given by Fouquet in honor of Louis XIV on August 17, 1661—so lavish that the superintendent of finances soon went to prison. Vatel himself had to flee to England. On returning to France he entered the service of the king's brother, styled Monsieur. Finally, in 1669, he began working for the Grand Condé as chief steward responsible for all provisions, from household to stables.

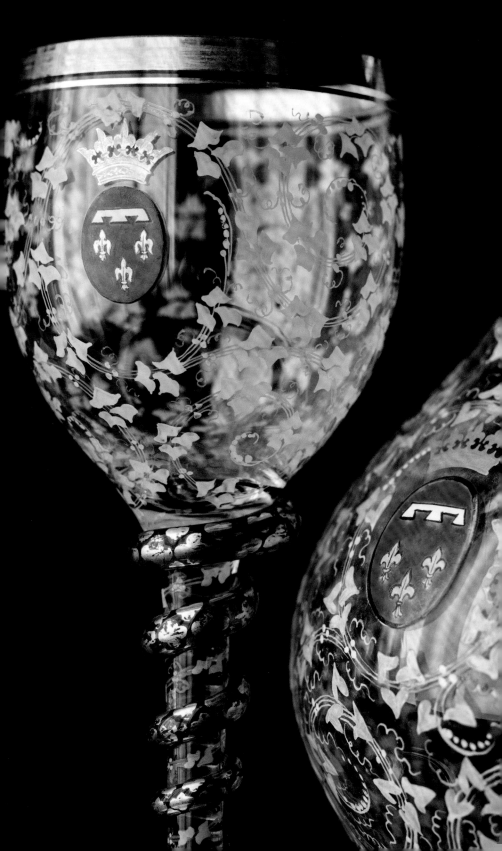

DÉJEUNER DU 28 Mars 1897

Oeufs pochés à la Dauphine

Brochet S^{ce} Mousseline

Poulet sauté aux Morilles

Selle de Pré salé S^{ce} poivrade

Chartreuse d'York à la Russe

Bécassines rôties

Salade de Romaine

Petits pois à l'Anglaise

Gateau Napolitain

LE RAPPORT

It so happened that three days of extraordinary festivities, on April 25–27, 1671, were planned in honor of the king, the queen, the king's brother, and the royal court. It was to be the final stage of the reconciliation between Louis XIV and his cousin, Condé. Vatel had worked around the clock to prepare for the arrival of nearly two thousand guests. Thanks to Madame de Sévigné's letters, we know that right from the first evening some tables lacked roast meat, due to the presence of unexpected guests. Vatel felt that he had been "dishonored," but the Grand Condé reassured him. Then the midnight fireworks were spoiled by clouds. For the meal on the second day, a Friday, Vatel had ordered fish from various ports in France. When the morning fish delivery didn't arrive, Vatel feared he would have nothing to serve the king; in despair, he went up to his room, wedged his sword in the door, and threw himself upon it—just as fish began arriving from all sides. Vatel the perfectionist, probably also suffering from the strain of preparing such an event, didn't think he could live with the shame. The Grand Condé was extremely dismayed, but the party carried on and was a great success. Vatel, meanwhile, was hastily buried that very day in the cemetery of the local parish church of Saint-Firmin.

Vatel's heroic suicide turned him into a legend. Many culinary innovations have subsequently been credited to him. But no, he did *not* invent the famous whipped cream known as crème Chantilly, which only dates back to the latter half of the eighteenth century. The delicious cream that would make Chantilly's gourmet reputation was first served when the Count and Countess of Nord (pseudonyms used by the future Tsar and Tsarina of Russia) paid a visit to the Prince of Condé in 1872. ∎

FACING PAGE
The table in the Stag Gallery is set
as it would have been in the days of the
Duke of Aumale. The Sèvres porcelain
bears the duke's monogram.
PAGES 138–39
A crystal glass with the duke's
monogram, sitting in a cooler.

TOP AND BOTTOM
Berthe of Clinchamp's
bathroom and bedroom.

Medallion portrait of Berthe,
Countess of Clinchamp, 1898.
The countess, one of the duke's
friends, wears the Starred Cross,
an Austrian decoration awarded
only to noblewomen.

The Incredible Painting Collection

Part of the fascination of the Condé Museum resides in the fact that no apparent logic governs the hanging of pictures. Gone is the chronological, educational approach that prevails all over France in regional museums devoted to the fine arts. The Duke of Aumale's own preferences, his desire to surprise his guests, and the stimulating pleasure of variety all guide the eye of museum-goers who here are neither tourists nor visitors but "guests."

This unique public museum, heir to the Louvre of the Revolutionary and Napoleonic periods, seemed provocative during the Third Republic (1870–1940). It was the last princely, eclectic, and highly personal collection to be assembled in France, comparable to the vast accumulations of masterpieces hanging—in an apparent disorder that is the height of elegance—in the British stately homes that the Duke of Aumale knew so well. At Chantilly, taking the time to look, and perhaps to launch into a discussion, can be done either on a central bench (as in other museums) or on small seats upholstered in red damask (as in a palace).

Paintings can be found everywhere at Chantilly, from the private apartments to the halls of the museum. More than sculpture, rare furniture, military trophies, or antiques, paintings truly reflect the duke's taste—as do his other personal penchants, namely drawings, books, and illuminated manuscripts, which are much harder to display. By acquiring only works of solid provenance—sometimes by buying an entire collection—and by taking advice from famous connoisseurs such as Frédéric Reiset, who was a curator at the Louvre and a friend of Ingres—the Duke of Aumale rarely made a mistake. For that matter, it was Reiset who sold the duke a collection of drawings, as well as, in 1879, forty paintings,

FACING PAGE
Jean-François de Troy, *Dining on Oysters*, 1735. This was the first painting to depict champagne.

PAGES 144–45
The "French wall" in the Gallery of Painting.

HISTORY MUSEUM
VERSUS ART MUSEUM

The Condé Museum is unique and uncategorizable. Its incredible collection of paintings can only be understood in light of its books and manuscripts, its drawings, and its archives. Nor can the collection be understood independently of the château that was largely devised and shaped for it—nor the château without the historic gardens flanking it, plus the stables, racetrack, and forest beyond.

So what was the Duke of Aumale's ambition when forging this museum? Various interpretations emerge from an apparent mélange of parallels and divergences. The duke—as the son of a king, as an historian, as a student of Michelet with great enthusiasm for his country's days of glory—was strongly influenced by his father's grand plan to establish a museum of French history in the château de Versailles. At Chantilly, the walls breathe history, the history not only of its previous owners but of the entire country. Portraiture therefore predominates, illustrating the duke's historic research, enhancing an understanding of his books and archives. Like the project launched by his father, all types of French political regime are reconciled here, from ancien-régime portraits to pictures of Napoleon, via the gallery of the Orléans family itself.

The family connection is obvious; the genealogical links resonate. Aumale had in mind the fabulous collection of the Orléans family in the Palais-Royal, sold by Philippe-Égalité. Like his father Louis-Philippe, the Duke of Aumale bought back a few superb relics. The hanging also pays tribute to his elder brother, Ferdinand, Duke of Orléans, a precocious admirer of Romantic and Orientalist paintings, several masterpieces of which are given pride of place in the château.

Yet Chantilly is above all the scene of extremely enriching, personal moments experienced by its last owner, marked by great accomplishments as well as deep mourning. It's almost like placing Italy on the banks of the little stream running through the grounds: Naples-on-Nonette. The Italian wall in the Gallery of Painting evokes the Italian roots of the duke's mother and wife, while the French wall opposite reflects the Orientalism of the soldier who defeated Abdelkader in Algeria, even as it hosts the large historic portraits and images of the war and fame he never really knew. Marked by his periods of exile, the duke developed a defense and illustration of the grand French style in his proud retreat of Chantilly, located outside—but not too distant from—the capital. It's like a passage in an opera—which the duke so loved—in which a unity of time and place merge with the unity of a man's plan and collection, reflecting his past as well as what was ultimately his thoroughly modern vision. ■

FACING PAGE
Alexandre-Gabriel Decamps,
Turkish Children Playing with a Tortoise
(detail), 1836.
PAGE 150
The rotunda in the Gallery of Painting,
showing Luca Penni's *Portrait of Henri II*,
Raphael's *Madonna of Loreto*, and Piero
di Cosimo's *Portrait of Simonetta Vespucci*.
PAGE 151
Piero di Cosimo, *Portrait of Simonetta
Vespucci*. The most beautiful woman in
Florence, who died prematurely in 1476,
inspired artists and poets.

including Piero di Cosimo's *Portrait of Simonetta Vespucci*, a panel from a wedding chest depicting a scene from the Book of Esther by Filippino Lippi and Sandro Botticelli, and modern paintings such as François Gérard's *Portrait of Bonaparte* and one of the finest nineteenth-century portraits of a woman, Ingres' *Madame Duvaucey*—and paintings by Nicolas Poussin.

Right from his first exile, the Duke of Aumale began collecting works that he hoped to display in France some day. His biographer, Raymond Cazelles, wrote that, "by the age of forty, [the duke] had put together the finest museum in England." The archives at Chantilly contain sketches of the hanging at Twickenham, and in his notebooks the duke recorded his purchases like so many military campaigns and victories. At the 1863 auction of the collection of Prince Demidov (the husband of Mathilde Bonaparte), he bought Ingres' *Stratonica,* a subtly colored painting that belies the myth that Ingres was exclusively a "draftsman"; it had been commissioned from Ingres by the duke's older brother, the Duke of Orléans. When the auctioneer brought his hammer down and announced that the Duke of Aumale, represented by an agent, was the highest bidder, the room burst into applause—in Paris itself, from which the Second Empire had banished the entire Orléans family. His collection was clearly also an instrument of status and politics.

Aumale recovered works that had hung in the Palais-Royal prior to the Revolution, and he also bought pieces once owned by his father, as well as those he liked from his elder brother's collection. He became master of the galleries of his father-in-law, the Prince of Salerno, and bought what he liked, with a personal taste for Orientalism, the French and Italian Renaissance, military history, and feminine beauty—ranging from the grisaille stained glass depicting the story of Psyche (originally from Écouen) to one of the most famous sixteenth-century French paintings of a woman at her bath (formerly thought to be Gabrielle d'Estrées, Henri IV's mistress). He was also drawn to the architectural rigor and intellectual appeal of paintings by Nicolas Poussin, that archetypical French artist: the duke bought an undisputed masterpiece— *The Massacre of the Innocents*—as well as six other works by Poussin. To offset this trend toward rigor, Aumale added flirtatious *fêtes galantes* and other paintings by Watteau, as well as Jean-François de Troy's *Dining on Oysters,*

FACING PAGE
Nicolas Poussin, *Massacre of the Innocents*, c. 1625. This features one of the most poignant depictions of a scream in French painting.

"One of my finest prerogatives, as a prince and a wealthy man, is to be able to encourage the arts."

Henri of Orléans, Duke of Aumale, in a letter in 1846

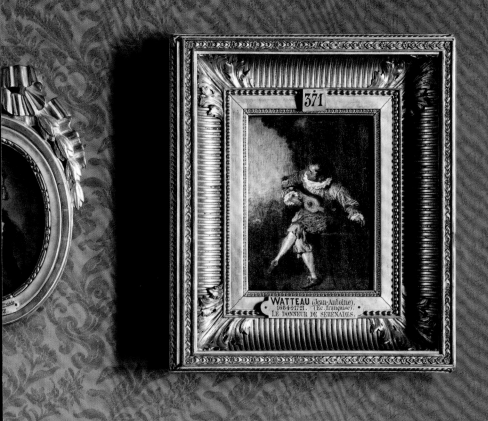

371

WATTEAU (Jean-Antoine).
1684 à 1721. (Éc. française).
LE DONNEUR DE SÉRÉNADES.

a perfect picture to show to guests, who tried to spot the soaring cork in this early depiction of a champagne bottle. In the Duke of Aumale's home, then, violence, war, and dreadful events existed side-by-side with images of frivolity and happiness.

The Condé Museum also pays tribute to other major collections: like the Uffizi in Florence, it contains a "Tribune" where favorite items from all periods are combined. The Santuario, meanwhile, shelters the most precious and fragile works from the light, employing a system of curtains to unveil, for example, Raphael's *Three Graces*. Above all, the museum boasts a magnificent Gallery of Painting, a mark of princely status that was also the origin of every public museum since the Grande Galerie was built in the Louvre. The hanging— which seemingly follows no clear rules apart from the division into two major walls, one French, one Italian—echoes what the duke had seen in other collections and what he had done himself at Twickenham. The house at Twickenham was near the stately home of another famous collector, Horace Walpole, who built Strawberry Hill House in a Gothic-revival vein. But Aumale had eyes only for the Renaissance, as expressed in his museum. He had a predilection for the work of Clouet father and son, assembling an impressive set of their paintings as well as a whole series of their drawings. (The Clouet collection was enhanced in the twentieth century by fine works from the Poncins-Biencourt collection—although the Condé Museum is not allowed to lend works, it can acquire new ones.) This museum thus features portraits of historical figures in France during the wars of religion, a period as disturbing as the one the duke himself experienced. Like his father, who had had Napoleon's remains brought back from Saint Helena and interred at the Invalides in Paris, Aumale admired the emperor. He bought *1805, Cuirassiers Before the Charge* by Jean-Louis-Ernest Meissonier, a painter of battles who was the most expensive artist of his day: barely visible, in the background, is the small figure of Napoleon in gray frock coat, commanding this charge. The gallery also shows the war lost by the French in 1870. Alphonse de Neuville, another great war artist, painted *Battle on the Railway*, which includes train tracks, rifles, and a telegraph pole—current developments were elevated to the level of old-master paintings like the nearby Carracci picture above the door.

THE POINT
OF THE TRIBUNE

In the museum patiently planned by the Duke of Aumale ever since his years of exile, each space plays its role. Near the Santuario (the home of smaller masterpieces) and the Gem Cabinet (*Cabinet des Gemmes,* a kind of treasure chamber) is the Tribune. Architecturally, the Tribune imitates the one found in the Uffizi Gallery in Florence, well known to the duke, which hosts masterpieces owned by the Medici family of Tuscany. Aumale instructed his architect, Daumet, to copy the same arrangement for showing his own masterworks. The high windows of the room in Florence, however, are replaced at Chantilly by Armand Bernard's paintings of places to which the duke was very attached. He wanted his Tribune to present a panorama of everything he loved about painting—it was *his* history of art, personal and perfect. Two walls are devoted to the Italian and Flemish Renaissance, with works by Fra Angelico, Botticelli, Perugino, and Titian. On the left are displayed the seventeenth- and eighteenth-century French and Flemish schools, including Poussin, van Dyck, Champaigne, and Watteau. The two final walls, facing one another, feature nineteenth-century French painting: on the left is the Romantic school, with remarkable paintings by Delaroche, Delacroix, and Scheffer, while on the opposite wall are four masterpieces by Ingres, including *Self-Portrait Aged Twenty Four*, begun in 1894 but poorly received by critics and later reworked by the artist. Nearby is Ingres's "Mona Lisa," that is to say his portrait of *Madame Duvaucey,* done during his stay at the Villa Medici in Rome in 1807; this, his finest portrait, molds the soft curves of the mistress of the French ambassador to the Holy See into a picture of ideal femininity. ∎

As a historian, Aumale liked sketches, the earliest versions of well-known works. He acquired a study by Antoine Jean Gros for *Plague Victims in Jaffa*, the first, very spare version of *Paolo and Francesca* by Ingres (who subsequently painted the subject many times), and a drawing of the *Nude Mona Lisa*. His interest in history and records spurred him to place portraits together (such as Richelieu and Mazarin), and to extend his collection of influential ministers to include Robert Nanteuil's pastel of Colbert and Ary Scheffer's portrait of Talleyrand (hanging in the Tribune). Indeed, Talleyrand played a role in the Prince of Condé's decision to become godfather and benefactor of the Duke of Aumale.

Although this museum is a conservatory of old France with its class distinctions, monarchs, and warriors, the ceiling of the main staircase, painted by Diogène Maillart to a design by Jules Élie Delaunay, celebrates the tricolored Republican flag. Aumale thus created his own personal pantheon. It is silly to criticize him for being unable to appreciate Courbet, Degas, Monet, and the impressionists, because his modernism was that of the Orientalists—the vast blue skies of Eugène Fromentin, or heavily impastoed, Rembrandt-like scenes by Alexandre Gabriel Decamps, an artist then at the height of his fame, whom Aumale boldly hung opposite his finest Poussin. His modernism extended to Corot and Rosa Bonheur, as impressed on his generation by contemporary publications now on the low bookshelves lining the gallery, namely magazines like *L'Artiste* and *La Gazette des Beaux-Arts*.

Nor did Aumale own Spanish paintings, which had been more to the taste of his father, King Louis-Philippe, who collected Velazquez, El Greco, and Murillo. When the king's personal collection was returned after the revolution of 1848, it was sold at auction, yet Aumale acquired nothing—true, he had just made other major purchases, but perhaps he refrained because he always preferred Italy, or because he was irritated by the Spanish fashions associated with Empress Eugénie. Nor did he own any Rubens, as though obeying the instructions given by Ingres—who adored Raphael— to his pupils: ignore Rubens. Although he had no Caravaggios, the duke owned a fine Caravaggio-like *Supper at Emmaus*, now attributed to French artist Trophime Bigot. He liked the Carraccis, and displayed a taste for Italian primitives and the French Renaissance, still little known in those days. In the Tribune he placed—alongside what he felt to be the finest works—a then-unidentified, highly poetic painting that turned out to be by Sassetta, a Sienese artist completely overlooked at the time. Whereas his father had turned the château de Versailles into a public museum devoted to "France's glorious past," the duke turned Chantilly into a princely collection open to all lovers of art and history. It was devoted first of all to the glory of the families who had owned the estate—the Montmorencys and the princes of Condé—but ultimately it coalesced, like a mosaic, into a portrait of himself.

In the Santuario he hung two Raphaels, *The Madonna of the House of Orléans* (which had belonged to his ancestors until it was sold by his grandfather, Philippe-Égalité) and *The Threes Graces,* that epitome of beauty. He surrounded them with the finest medieval illuminations by Jean Fouquet, taken from a book of hours. How did he decide where to place all these treasures? That's a secret he never revealed. It is up to beholders to take a good look, to intuit and reflect, to take their time. Perhaps he arranged the French pictures in the gallery to create, from one painting to the next, a kind of architectural continuity: a series of arches follows from Delacroix's *Two Foscaris* to Decamps's *Turkish Children* and Gros's *Plague Victims in Jaffa.* Meanwhile, a symmetry of skies is established between Fromentin and Corot—perhaps a deliberate effect, given the glass ceiling. On the "second row," above, draped fabrics echo one another, from Cardinal Mazarin's gown (painted by Champaigne) to Mademoiselle de Clermont's dress (by Nattier), creating a strange tricolor harmony, a blue-white-red effect visually reflected in a portrait of Louis XV in coronation robes alongside a portrait of Richelieu. Maybe the duke behaved like a painter when arranging his pictures, using them like pigments on a palette. At Chantilly, the collection itself is a work of art. ■

RAPHAEL

The Condé Museum boasts the largest collection, after the Louvre, of paintings and drawings by Raphael. The Duke of Aumale placed Raphael at the top of his personal pantheon. As an admirer of Ingres, he inevitably appreciated Raphael, and never failed to seek out the artist's masterpieces during his various travels.

After having bought, in 1861, the Reiset collection of drawings, which included many Raphaels, in 1869 the duke purchased a family icon, *The Madonna of the House of Orléans.* Painted in Florence circa 1506–7, this picture's superb modesty is astonishing. Set in a thoroughly humble interior, the Madonna's face glows with maternal love as she tenderly holds her son, who looks straight at the beholder with gentle earnestness. The primary colors, arranged with simple harmony, contrast with the dark background where we glimpse a remarkable, Flemish-inspired still life. The duke's other major acquisition, what he called "an exquisite gem," is undoubtedly Raphael's *Three Graces.* This very small panel was one of the master's first secular works, painted around 1503–4, when he was barely twenty. It is traditionally interpreted as the Three Graces—Aglaea (Splendor), Thalia (Abundance), and Euphrosyne (Joy), who notably incarnate Love, Beauty, and Chastity—even though the gold balls allude to the Hesperides, the nymphs from whom Hercules stole the golden apples. Analysis using infrared reflectography reveals that only one of the Graces—the one on the left—originally held an apple, while the one in the middle placed both hands on the shoulders of her companions and the third hid her genitals in the modest gesture used by

Venus. It was probably a quest for balance, for perfect harmony, that ultimately prompted Raphael to include the three golden fruits. The interplay of curves and radiant bodies turns these nudes into one of the earliest accomplished works by the young master, surpassing his predecessors. This precious treasure is enhanced by a Renaissance-revival frame of chased, repoussé silver commissioned from gold-smiths Froment-Meurice in 1890, coinciding with completion of work on the Santuario. *The Madonna of the House of Orléans*, meanwhile, was set in an ebony frame made by the same firm.

There is a final twist to this wonderful story: the duke acquired his first Raphael without realizing it. In 1854, he bought the collection of his father-in-law, the Prince of Salerno, which included *The Madonna of Loreto*, considered a copy at the time. In a magnificently maternal gesture, simultaneously serious and resigned, the Madonna (accompanied by a Saint Joseph added later), wraps the sculptural yet lively baby Jesus in her sheer veil. The child seems to accept this prefiguration of his shroud—indeed, he plays with it. Study and restoration of the painting, carried out in the 1970s, revealed not only its quality but also the figure 133, corresponding to the inventory number of the Borghese collection to which it belonged in the late seventeenth century. This sensational revelation conclusively consolidated the Condé collection's essential contribution to our understanding of Raphael, that Renaissance genius. ■

FACING PAGE
Raphael, *The Madonna of Loreto*.
It was only in the 1970s that
this painting was discovered to
be an original Raphael.

The Drawing Collection

Stored in a theater that the Duke of Aumale transformed into a library are over four thousand drawings, protected from the light by being meticulously placed in red portfolios classified by school. It is one of the finest collections of drawings in the world.

The duke inherited just a few portrait drawings of his family and some historic documents on Chantilly. It was in England, during his twenty-three years of exile, that he put together a wonderful collection of drawings, following in the footsteps of great collectors like Mariette and Crozat. Although advised by Triqueti and Reiset, Aumale relied above all on his own eye and taste. That taste led him toward historic portraits, notably those of previous owners of Chantilly. His first purchase was in fact a portrait of Louis, first prince of Condé, although that identification later proved mistaken. Several decades later, in 1876, he acquired a collection of historic portraits assembled by Alexandre Lenoir, including masterpieces by Clouet, Dumonstier, and Nanteuil. These efforts were capped in 1889 by his purchase, from Lord Carlisle, of no fewer than 311 portrait drawings by Jean and François Clouet and their studio. That extraordinary collection, assembled by the queen of France, Catherine de' Medici, had been labeled by the queen and her secretaries, making it possible to reconstruct life at the court of the Valois kings with its pomp and its intrigues. The duke thus brought one of the treasures of French art back to France even as he established, along with drawings he already owned, the world's leading collection of French Renaissance portraiture, namely the henceforth-famous 366 sheets of the "Chantilly Clouets."

FACING PAGE
Raphael, *Half-Clothed Man Carrying a Burden*, sketch in red chalk for the fresco *The Coronation of Charlemagne* in the Vatican.

Sapata

FACING PAGE AND ABOVE
Jean Clouet, *François 1er*, c. 1524
and *Léonore de Sapata*, c. 1531.

THE DRAWING COLLECTION **173**

"The Leonardo arrived yesterday.
I was away, and didn't allow it to be
unpacked until this morning, early. After
briefly possessing it, my first concern is
not to give you my impressions—which
would take too long—but to tell you
how happy I am to own this masterpiece,
and how grateful I am to you for
arranging the purchase."

The Duke of Aumale to Henri de Triqueti, regarding the *Nude Mona Lisa*, February 15, 1862

The duke's diaries reveal his great fondness for the Renaissance, in both its French and Italian forms. In the late 1860s he bought the collection of Frédéric Reiset, an eminent curator of drawings—and later, paintings—at the Louvre. It comprised nearly 380 drawings, including 150 by masters of the Italian Renaissance (Raphael, Michelangelo, Parmigianino, Primaticcio, and so on) as well as by Dürer, Rubens, van Dyck, Poussin, Lorrain, Watteau, and others. He pulled off a coup in 1862 by acquiring, for the sum of 7,000 francs, a notorious *Nude Mona Lisa*, then attributed to Leonardo da Vinci. On February 15, beside himself with joy, he wrote to Triqueti: "The Leonardo arrived yesterday. I was away, and didn't allow it to be unpacked until this morning, early. After briefly possessing it, my first concern is not to give you my impressions—which would take too long—but to tell you how happy I am to own this masterpiece, and how grateful I am to you for arranging the purchase." Recent scientific analysis, combined with renewed art historical research, has demonstrated that this large sketch, whose watermarks point to Leonardo's Italy, was the work of a creative, left-handed artist who mastered Leonardo's technique and produced a design used in his studio. The drawing, nearly the same size as the *Mona Lisa*, shows a nude woman from the waist up, in the same pose as her cousin in the Louvre, but more suggestive of Venus. It can be attributed to Leonardo's studio, indeed probably to the master himself.

Chantilly's collection of drawings also extends to Orientalist works, appreciated by a man who played a major role in France's Algerian campaign in the 1840s. In 1864, artist Adrien Dauzats served as the duke's agent when purchasing, at the posthumous sale of Delacroix's estate, one of the seven sketchbooks Delacroix filled during his trip to Morocco, dated 1832. The lively watercolors it contains are a constant marvel, notably his studies of young Jewish women done from life, and the superb landscapes he encountered during his travels.

The insatiable duke liked to acquire entire collections (which was also the case with books). In 1877, he managed to bag the whole society that once gathered around the Orléans family in the Palais-Royal in the late eighteenth century, immortalized in 484 watercolor portraits by Louis Carrogis Carmontelle. In 1880, Aumale added nearly six hundred drawings by Raffet and other war artists to his collection.

A print and drawing collection worthy of the name must also have its good share of prints. The nearly five thousand prints owned by the duke are first rank. As with drawings, historical portraits were of particular interest to the duke, as well as masterful Renaissance engravings by the likes of Dürer, Raimondi, and Duvet. Also noteworthy are engravings by Callot, some extraordinary Rembrandts, and works by Géricault.

As a friend of eminent curators at both the Bibliothèque Nationale and the Louvre, the duke asked them to catalog his collection. The goal was to produce a comprehensive catalog, but this unfulfilled ambition is still being pursued today to allow these treasures to become better known. They can currently be consulted by scholars, and also are exhibited in rotation, on a four-month basis, in the new prints and drawing room of the Condé Museum, opened in 2017. The creative process of some of the greatest artists can also be glimpsed in the fragile works on paper hung in the duke's guest bedrooms, restored to convey their intimate atmosphere. ■

ABOVE
Rembrandt, *Landscape with Mill in the Center (View of Dordrecht)*.
PAGES 178–79
Eugène Delacroix, Moroccan sketchbook. *Portraits of Jewish Women*, 1832.

THE DUKE OF AUMALE
AND PHOTOGRAPHY

People are often unaware that the Duke of Aumale was an early fan of a very new but very promising art—photography. During his exile in England, he learned to appreciate the budding medium among London's pioneering circles (which included Prince Albert). He acquired an impressive collection of nearly two thousand prints. The pride of the collection comprises early French photographers—he owned five superb seascapes by Gustave Le Gray and views of Paris by Édouard Denis Baldus. As an exile, the duke found it the perfect way to keep abreast of the changes to Paris being made by Baron Haussmann and Napoleon III, notably to the Louvre and Tuileries Palaces, both of which he had known in his youth. And as a tireless traveler, Aumale also wanted to acquire photographs of cities he knew, notably Rome and Athens, while his nephew Robert, Duke of Chartres, practiced amateur photography in southern Italy and Sicily.

The gems in this outstanding collection also include early war pictures, in particular about fifty prints by Roger Fenton documenting the 1855 Crimean War between the Russian Empire and a coalition formed by France, the United Kingdom, the Kingdom of Sardinia, and the Ottoman Empire. Similarly, he acquired several photographs of the American Civil War, in which two of his nephews—the Count of Paris and the Duke of Chartres—fought. Photographs also helped to document his art collection, thanks to the acquisition of reproductions of artworks in other museums and collections, which served as points of comparison. The medium also made it possible to exchange small carte-de-visite portraits and to compile family albums—Chantilly's photo collection reveals the extent to which the Duke of Aumale was the hub of a dense web of royal and princely families across Europe. ■

The Library

Architect Honoré Daumet designed the Duke of Aumale's Library (*Cabinet des Livres*) in the spirit of those found in British stately homes, featuring an upper gallery, warm wood paneling, and a ceiling decorated with the coats of arms of companions of the Grand Condé, whose bust (by Antoine Coysevox) overlooks the room. A painting by Gabriel Ferrier, placed on an easel next to the duke's comfortable armchair, makes it easy to imagine the hours he spent here reading and chatting to Alfred Auguste Cuvillier-Fleury, who had been his childhood tutor and taught him to love old books. Cuvillier-Fleury, historian and literary critic, an admirer of both Lamartine and Victor Hugo, and a friend of Alexandre Dumas fils, officially inducted the Duke of Aumale into the Académie Française in 1873. In his welcoming speech, he referred to Aumale as "Monsieur" for the first time, having always addressed the duke as "Your Highness" ever since Louis-Philippe hired him as a tutor for his son, despite the king's advice that, "Princes should be brought up as though they weren't."

The Library of nearly twenty thousand volumes, including fifteen hundred manuscripts, is a treasure hoard for booklovers, whom Aumale often invited to share his passion. He was proud to be a historian among others, valued for his recent, scholarly publications, in an equality that he had experienced at public school and was pleased to find again at the Institut de France.

Exhibitions are held in the Library to display the riches of a collection that includes illuminated manuscripts from the Middle Ages and the Renaissance, incunabula, and original, often unique, editions of authors the duke appreciated. He brought an expert eye, sensitive to the refinement of paintings in medieval manuscripts, to books, whose history he sought to trace back through major collections. When it came to printed books, he was alert to the quality of printing and the rarity of bindings. His was the rarest and most valuable private library of the day.

FACING PAGE
The Library holds nearly twenty thousand manuscripts and rare books.

PAGES 184–85
A bust of the Grand Condé overlooks the Library. The painting on the right shows the Duke of Aumale with his tutor and friend, Alfred Cuvillier-Fleury, who was a member of the Académie Française.

PAGES 186–87
Two illuminated manuscripts, *Tristan en prose*, with the coat of arms of Montmorency, Condé Museum's Library, and *Liber Floridus*, ms 724, among many others preserved in Chantilly.

PAGES 188–89
A mechanical chair owned by the Duke of Bourbon, who was the last prince of Condé and the Duke of Aumale's godfather.

xv

Michael archangelus
pugnat cū dracone
et angeli ei̇ cum eo

Nūc fcū est salus
et vūs et regnū
dei nāi et potestas
christi eius

A second, larger library was built in 1889 on the spot where a theater stood in the days of the duke's godfather. It contains thirty thousand volumes and now also houses the drawing collection. As a working library, it holds many history books as well as documents from the days of the Fronde, the Wars of Religion, the French Revolution, and the French Empire, not to mention more recent works by the likes of Victor Hugo, the Goncourt brothers, and Émile Zola, occasionally bearing a handwritten dedication by the author. Since 1898, a small reading room set aside for scholars has made it possible, in an ever-growing library, to pursue the serious research that the founder of these premises hoped to encourage after he was gone. ■

BELOW
The Duke of Aumale's membership card to the French Booklovers' Society for the years 1888–89.
FACING PAGE
A full-length photograph of the Duke of Aumale standing by a bookshelf.

1888   1889

SOCIÉTÉ DES BIBLIOPHILES FRANÇAIS
S. A. R. Monseigneur le Duc d'Aumale.

Dec. Janv. Fev. Mars. Avr. Mai.
12   9   13   13   10   8
26   23   27   27   24   22

THE *TRÈS RICHES HEURES DU DUC DE BERRY*

The most famous book of the Middle Ages is a beautifully illuminated manuscript, the *Très Riches Heures du Duc de Berry* (The Very Rich Hours of the Duke of Berry). It is cataloged at Chantilly, like others, under a shelfmark that serves as its code-name: Ms 65. The book is the most valuable work in the Condé Museum, the one of which the duke was proudest, and is kept in a safe (the Library holds a facsimile). The duke was only thirty-three when he managed to buy it from a collector in Genoa in 1856. He allowed his wife to open the crate when the precious shipment arrived at Twickenham—he had immediately recognized it in Italy when leafing through it, thanks to the coat of arms and portrait of the Duke of Berry, plus views of Vincennes and Mount Saint-Michel. The manuscript suited the duke in every way: it had belonged to the extravagant third son of King John the Good, an art patron and collector, one of those "fleur-de-lis princes" who, not being in line for the throne, decided to devote themselves to the arts and grand architectural projects. The Duke of Aumale identified with the Duke of Berry, and was also fascinated by King John, held captive in England after the battle of Poitiers in 1356; he had even published on John, in whom he perhaps saw a reflection of his own father, Louis-Philippe, also subjected to exile.

Commissioned around 1410 from brothers Pol, Johan, and Herman Limbourg, then completed by other great artists throughout the fifteenth century, the book is divided into several sections: its famous calendar, in which each month is illustrated by a building; four excerpts from the Gospels illustrated by large symbolic plates, the most beautiful depicting the vision of Saint John on Patmos; prayers to the Virgin, psalms, and other prayers to be recited (the litany of saints, hours of the Cross, hours of the Holy Ghost); the office of the dead, the weekday offices, the hours of the Passion of Christ (with a magnificent nocturnal scene); and, finally, a series of pages devoted to the major feasts of the liturgical year. The dazzle of lapis-lazuli blue and pink lake, the subtle palette of greens, and the sparing use of gold impart a visual unity to this manuscript, right up to its completion by artist Jean Colombe (died 1493) while it was owned by the Duke of Savoy. ■

FACING PAGE
Limbourg brothers, *Zodiacal Man*,
miniature from the *Très Riches Heures
du Duc de Berry*.

PAGES 194–95
The month of February from the *Très
Riches Heures du Duc de Berry*.

PAGES 196–97
The Library in the former theater, holding
the Duke of Aumale's working volumes.

					feuuier a xxviij jours et la lune xxix.	la finite des jours	le nõb. voz.
							nouel viij.
						xlv.	
						ix.	xluj.	xui.
					saint bride.	iiij.	luij.	
					La purification.	v.		ij.
ij.	d	f	kl		saint blaise.	v.	xv.	x.
ix.	e	f		ponas	saint auertin.	x.	xv.	xviij.
	f	vij	id		sainte agathe.	x.	xbij.	
vij.	g	vij	id		saint amant.	x.	xxi.	vij.
	A	vij	id		saint romain.	x.	xxij.	
xbi.	b	vij	id		saint salomon.	x.	xxiij.	xbi.
	c	vij	id		saint apoline.	x.	xxbj.	iiij.
iiij.	d	iiij	id		sainte scolastique.	x.	xxx.	
	e	iij	id		saint desir.	x.	xxxiij.	uij.
xij.	f	ij	id		sainte eulalie.	x.	xxxbj.	
j.	g		Jdus.		saint iulian.	x.	xxxix.	ix.
	A	xbi	kl		Saint valentin.	x.	xlij.	
xbiij.	b	xbi	kl		saint maurel.	x.	xlv.	xbij.
bij.	c	xb	kl		sainte uiuienne.	x.	xlbij.	
	d	xiiij	kl		saint donace.	x.	uij.	bi.
vb.	e	xiij	kl		saint symeon.	x.	x.	viij.
iiij.	f	xij	kl		sainte felanine.	ij.	bi.	
	g	xi	kl		saint eleuther.	ij.	ix.	
xij.	A	x.			saint victor.	ij.	xij.	x.
j.	b	ix	kl		saint pierre.	ij.	xv.	
	c	viij	kl		saint poliraus.	ij.	xbij.	
xbiij	d	vij	kl		saint mathyas.	ij.	xx.	
	e	vi	kl		saint victorin.	ij.	xxiij.	
bij.	f	v.	kl		sainte uenice.			
xbiij	g	iiij	kl		saint honoure.			
bj.	A	iij	kl		saint iust.			
	b	ij.						
iiij								

THE THEFT OF
THE PINK DIAMOND

One night in October 1926, two thieves broke into the Connétable's Tower, fitted out and decorated to serve as a treasury. They crossed the moat and used ladders to get in through a window. At the time it was called the "Jewel Tower," to evoke the riches in the Tower of London. All the jewelry, miniatures, and precious objects that the Duke of Aumale had collected in tribute to the House of Orléans and the princes of Condé were displayed there. The thieves seized weapons studded with gems as well as a legendary pink diamond named after the Grand Condé. The 9.01-carat stone came from the Golconda mines in India. Cut into a pear shape, it had a slight irregularity on one side that made it recognizable anywhere; it was allegedly brought to France as a gift to King Louis XIV by a famous traveler, Jean-Baptiste Tavernier. The king reportedly gave it to his cousin, the Grand Condé, and so this legendary gem was handed down in the family until it reached the Duke of Aumale's godfather. Listed among the property at Chantilly as early as 1720, it was later set on an insignia of the Order of the Golden Fleece, thereby rivaling the insignia worn by Louis XV, featuring the royal French Blue diamond. Then the Duke of Aumale's mother, Queen Maria Amelia, apparently had one of her favorite jewelers, Bapst, set it on a pin. The duke turned it into a museum piece. Nothing stolen in October 1926 was ever found—except the pink diamond (and a yellow diamond), hidden in an apple. The chambermaid at the hotel where the thieves were arrested had bitten into it, unwittingly succumbing to the lure of diamonds. Nowadays a copy is placed in the display case, while the diamond—like the *Très Riches Heures*—is kept in a safe. ■

FACING PAGE
The pink diamond's amazing color
and shape are unique.

A Lesson in Garden History

From the top steps of the Jeu de Paume (indoor tennis hall), the Duke of Aumale could gaze upon a tree-framed vista worthy of the *Très Riches Heures du Duc de Berry,* including his irregularly shaped château with its bristling towers and chapel with lofty steeple. It was a landscape he had drawn himself, a modern illuminated page that vaunted ecology before its time. Some thirty miles (fifty kilometers) from Paris, the forest of Chantilly serves as protective setting for grounds that, like a living museum, recount the entire history of French gardens.

In the seventeenth century, André Le Nôtre laid out the main lines of the grounds. Le Nôtre wrote that, of all the gardens he designed, Chantilly was his favorite. He devised a machine to lift water, found in abundance here, and established the principal lanes and overall architecture. He was assisted by Jean-Baptiste La Quintinie, who oversaw the king's fruit and vegetable gardens at Versailles. Chantilly's originality stems from the fact that its major compositional lines did not extend from the château, which remained surrounded by moats, as in medieval times. Thus the

BACKGROUND IMAGE
Adam Pérelle, *The Cascades at the Top of the Small Wood* (detail).

LEFT
Adam Pérelle, *Overall View of Chantilly from the Entrance,* late seventeenth century.

FACING PAGE
In the landscape garden, the Isle of Love was set where the princes of Condé once organized summer festivities. This little island, ringed with fountains and box hedges, features a kiosk that houses the statue of Eros.

PAGES 202–3
Adam Pérelle, *The Orangery Parterre.* This was the first part of the grounds to be laid out by André Le Nôtre.

PAGES 204–5
View of the château from the landscape garden.

PAGES 206–7
A late seventeenth-century gouache depicting festivities in the formal gardens designed by André Le Nôtre.

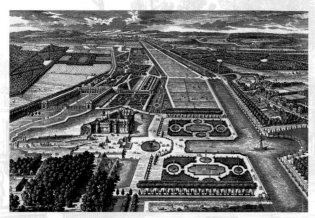

reflecting pool that runs symmetrically up to the entrance gates mirrors only sky, not architecture. At the end of the long vista, a wide canal heads, at a right angle, toward a large, spectacular cascade. Unlike Versailles, no single, central viewpoint predominates over others. Instead, multiple angles offer new perspectives to be discovered during a promenade.

As a guest of the Duchess of Montmorency, poet Théophile de Viau (1590–1626) wrote some of his finest verses in "the house of Sylvia" (named after the wood nymph). This little retreat was preserved, and the Duke of Aumale had it restored and enlarged, in perhaps his finest gesture of interest in the history of the grounds. In fact, Chantilly is also a literary garden, echoing the Library, thanks to statues of Molière and La Fontaine, set up according to the duke's wishes.

In the eighteenth century, when owned by the princes of Condé, Chantilly had its own hamlet, predating Versaille's Petit Trianon, complete with whimsical farm and famous "surprise thatched cottage" that masked a palace. Prior to the French Revolution, Chantilly boasted all the features that delighted European garden lovers, from a maze to an "Anglo-Chinese" garden. These features were renovated in the nineteenth century and still survive today. The Duke of Aumale liked to stroll there in the afternoon, in the warm sunshine, book in hand.

The landscape garden, laid out when the princes of Condé returned to Chantilly during the Bourbon Restoration, is typical of nineteenth-century garden design with curves imitating nature and follies appearing on the horizon. Its bridge celebrating great men, Isle of Love, and Temple of Venus were all inspired by the Trianon. The grounds also have sports facilities such as an archery range, a Petit Parc (Little Park) with beehives, a life-size game of Shoots and Ladders for kids and even a "kangaroo enclosure"—indeed, the Duke of Aumale's son, the Prince of Condé, was an early French explorer of Australia. Perpetuating this tradition, every year Chantilly holds a famous flower show that attracts everyone interested in the art of gardening, where specialists the world over come to meet and greet. ■

BACKGROUND IMAGE
François Denis Née, *View of the Château and Gardens of Chantilly, from the Top of the Sloping Greensward* (detail).
FACING PAGE
The Hamlet, inaugurated in 1775.
PAGES 210–11
The raised terrace designed by Daniel Gittard.
PAGES 212–13
Snow dusts the patterned greenery in the Aviary Garden.

The Life of a Timeless Museum

"Desirous of preserving for France the estate of Chantilly in its entirety, with its woods, lawns, waters, and buildings and everything they contain, including trophies, paintings, books, archives, and objets d'art, everything that constitutes a complete, varied monument to every sphere of French art and to the history of my country during its days of glory, I have decided to leave it to an illustrious institution that has honored me by doubly calling me to its ranks, and which, without ignoring the inevitable transformation of society, remains aloof from factional strife and sudden upheavals, retaining its independence throughout political fluctuations."

This wonderful statement is the preamble to the Duke of Aumale's will, drawn up on June 3, 1884. This bequest to the Institut de France, transformed into a gift with right of usufruct in 1886, became effective upon his death on May 7, 1897. The bequest imposed very strict conditions regarding respect for the display and hanging devised by the duke, as well as a prohibition on lending artworks.

Chantilly was the home of one of the world's greatest collectors. It is also an age-old aristocratic dwelling imbued with French history as experienced by a series of grand dynastic houses: Bouteiller de Senlis, Orgement, Montmorency, and finally Condé. Time seems to have come to a halt here, preserving a unique, authentic record of a singular history and vision.

The modern museum founded by the Duke of Aumale, named the Condé Museum in honor of his predecessors, remains immutable. Spectacular renovations have nevertheless been carried out in recent years, notably on

FACING PAGE
The main staircase is crowned by a painting, *Hope*, by Diogène Maillart (c. 1892), after a sketch by Jules Élie Delaunay.
PAGES 216–17
This tapestry, woven at Beauvais after a cartoon by Jean-François de Troy, overlooks a magnificent ironwork banister by the Moreau brothers.

Le Nôtre's gardens, the Grand Apartments, the Singeries, the Gallery of Painting, the Private Apartments of the Duke and Duchess of Aumale, and the roof of the Great Stables. Ambitious temporary exhibitions are held in the Jeu de Paume, while the establishment of a department of prints and drawings has made it possible to see the collection's priceless works on paper. Yet there remains much to be done to enable this extraordinary heritage—one of humanity's real treasures—to continue to cast its sparkling spell. ∎

LEFT
One of the stained glass from the *Cupid and Psyche* series (detail).
FACING PAGE
The façade overlooking the Aviary Garden features busts of Roman emperors.
PAGES 220–21
The statue of Eros beneath the trelliswork on the Isle of Love.

Acknowledgments

Mathieu Deldicque and Adrien Goetz would like to thank
Nicole Garnier, Senior Curator of Heritage, Condé Museum;
Marie-Pierre Dion, Senior Curator, Library and Archives, Condé Museum;
Marina Rouyer, Assistant Curator, Condé Museum;
Florent Picouleau, Assistant Archivist, Condé Museum;
and the entire team at the Domaine de Chantilly.

Photographic Credits

FACING PAGE
Detail of a decorative mask
beneath the main staircase.

PAGE 224
A fanciful coat of arms for the
Duke of Aumale on a firescreen
in the Condé Salon.

EDITORIAL DIRECTOR
Suzanne Tise-Isoré
Collection Style & Design

EDITORIAL COORDINATION
Léonie Piraudeau

GRAPHIC DESIGN
Bernard Lagacé

TRANSLATION FROM THE FRENCH
Deke Dusinberre

COPY EDITING AND PROOFREADING
Lindsay Porter

PRODUCTION
Corinne Trovarelli

COLOR SEPARATION
Les Artisans du Regard, Paris

PRINTED BY
C&C Offset, China

Simultaneously published in French as *Un jour à Chantilly*
English-language edition
© Flammarion, S.A., Paris, 2020

Flammarion S.A.
87, quai Panhard-et-Levassor
75647 Paris cedex 13
editions.flammarion.com
styleetdesign-flammarion.com

20 21 22 3 2 1
ISBN: 9782080204370
Legal deposit: 10/2020